The Flavor
of
Chinatown

唐人街味風

The Flavor
of
Chinatown

by
Brian St. Pierre and Jennie Low

Chronicle Books • San Francisco

We wish to express our appreciation to Lauan Garnjost, who participated in this project from the very beginning. She assisted in doing research, evaluating restaurants, and taste-testing recipes. She also helped with proofreading and typing.

Copyright © 1982 by Brian St. Pierre and Jennie Low

Library of Congress Cataloging in Publication Data
St. Pierre, Brian.
    The flavor of Chinatown.
    Includes index.
    1. San Francisco (Calif.) — Restaurants — Directories.
2. Chinatown (San Francisco, Calif.) — Restaurants — Directories. 3. San Francisco (Calif.) — Stores, shopping centers, etc. — Directories. 4. Chinatown (San Francisco, Calif.) — Stores, shopping centers, etc. — Directories. 5. San Francisco (Calif.) — Markets — Directories. 6. Chinatown (San Francisco, Calif.) — Markets — Directories. I. Low, Jennie, 1940–   . II. Title.
TX907.S7   1982   647'.9579461   82-14556
ISBN: 0-87701-261-X

Book and cover design by Thomas Ingalls
Composition by Accent & Alphabet
Illustrations by Tom Wilson

Chronicle Books
870 Market Street
San Francisco, CA 94102

Our deepest appreciation goes to these fearless chopstickers, none of whom were hungry an hour later . . .

THE BEAN-CURD HERD

Theresa Ballou
Esther Bateman
Joe Belden
Judy Berkley (Medal of Valor)
George and Marilyn Carleton
Mack Chrysler
Julia Crookstone
Samuel L. Deitsch, Jr.
Donna Ewald
Margene Fudenna
Alan and Erni Goldman
Steve and Cindy Grauer
Ailie Knorr
Bill and Eileen LeBlond
Cindy Low
Denise Low
Kelly McCune
Mike and Peg Mee
Maria Nelson
Marshall Newman
Norwood and Charlot Pratt
Jim Seff (Oak Leaf Cluster)
Larry Smith
Doong Tien

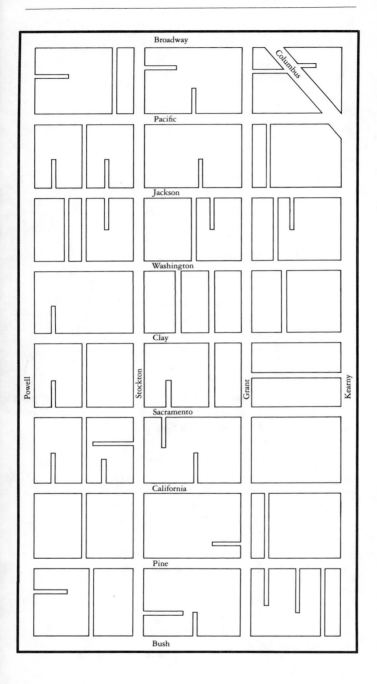

Table of Contents

*The Flavor
of
Chinatown*

Introduction

There were Chinese in San Francisco before the gold rush in 1849, though it was many years before they were able to found anything like a community, and most of the early immigrants were from Canton.

They came to escape the bloody aftermath of a lost war, and though conditions here were harsh, and discrimination systematic and unremitting, it was better than they had left behind, at least for a while. They built the railroads, reclaimed the Sacramento River Delta land, and provided the cheap labor that gave California a broad industrial base; in return, they were denied the right to testify in court, mine gold, apply for citizenship, or bring in their families—at the end of 1851, there were twelve thousand Chinese men in San Francisco, and seven Chinese women. A Chinese character in John Steinbeck's *East of Eden* explains:

> A man and a woman and a baby have a way of digging in, of pulling the earth where they are about them and scratching out a home. And then it takes all hell to root them out. But a crowd of men, nervous, lusting, restless, half sick with loneliness for women—why, they'll go anywhere, and particularly will they go home.

But there is a tenacity in the Chinese character that bad laws and worse people couldn't defeat; northern California prospered by their sweat and blood, and they would persist. People had to eat and have clean clothes, and merchants were always welcome, so the Chinese would cook and clean and import and retail and endure.

The original San Francisco Chinatown was a ghetto, strictly defined by law, cramped and crowded into the area between California and Pacific, and Stockton and Kearny: ten square blocks.

It was always pictured as some sort of microcosm of China, but in reality Chinatown has always been an odd sort of re-creation, a unique and foreign American community whose colorful quaintness often stoically obscured desperate poverty and overcrowding.

The earthquake and fire in 1906 destroyed Chinatown, and the rebuilding cured some of its worst ills. In 1911, the Manchu dynasty, exemplars of tyranny and corruption who had misruled China and extended their hold to Chinese in America, was overthrown; one result was a renewed sense of pride and independence for the Chinese people — though they still had a long way to go, many Chinese in America now felt they had some choices in their destiny.

In time the boundaries of Chinatown were extended down to Bush Street and up to Broadway, and over one block to Powell. Restaurants began to cater to tourists, sometimes grudgingly, and the character of the place changed yet again. After the Second World War, the discriminatory laws were finally abolished, and soon Chinatown became somewhat moribund as younger people moved away and joined the mainstream of California life and work.

In 1965, Lyndon Johnson lifted immigration quotas, and there was a flood of Chinese into the United States, many of whom settled in San Francisco — often being reunited with families who had been trying to bring them in for many years. Many of the new settlers came from Hong Kong, which had been a staging area for immigration to America. They didn't speak much English, and so Chinatown seemed the place to settle, where they'd be comfortable. They brought with them the immigrant's fierce desire to succeed, combined with a sophistication about food and urban survival that previous generations had lacked, and while they brought a host of problems and intracultural antagonisms, they also revitalized the restaurant business and had an impact on our society that goes far beyond the borders of Chinatown or even California.

Today, Chinatown is a little frayed but still supple—to paraphrase Mao, it bends with the winds of change. New restaurants and fabric shops and other stores open, and others are renovated. Stockton Street is an open-air bazaar on weekends, nicknamed "little Hong Kong." Like other neighborhoods around town, it is being plugged up by savings and loan associations and, though there isn't yet a McDonald's, there is an Orange Julius.

It will survive that, as it will survive, one hopes, Chinese kids drinking Seven-Up instead of tea with their meals; it carries the responsibility for the invention of fortune cookies and chop suey well, and is far less inscrutable than legend has it. Chinatown is a marvelous resource, a delightful adventure right in our own back yard.

You ought not to miss it.

A Glossary of Chinese Foods

As huge as China is, in both area and population, only a small proportion of its land is arable and can support any sort of food crop; if China were landlocked, its people would starve. The necessity caused by this brutal reality has been the mother of culinary invention of the highest order: nothing goes to waste, everything is used somehow. This ingenuity extends to a multitude of ingredients and preservation methods, as well as marvelous ways to restore or enhance flavors. There are many thousands of recipes in the Chinese repertoire, with uncountable permutations of ingredients. Here is a sampling of basics.

BAMBOO SHOOTS

Bamboo shoots are only sold in cans; their flavor is subtle, and they add a crunchy texture to stir-fried dishes. Always buy them whole, packed in water. Winter bamboo shoots (Companion brand) are smaller, crisper, and have more flavor than spring bamboo shoots, but they are rather more expensive. Avoid the presliced kind or the braised and seasoned version.

Leftover chunks should be kept in a jar, in fresh water changed every three days, in the refrigerator. They will keep for two weeks.

BEAN CAKE (Tofu)

The chameleon of Chinese food, tofu takes on the color and flavor of whatever it is cooked with. Made from soybeans, it is bland, very high in protein, low in calories, and quite inexpensive; it is used in a wide variety of dishes.

There are two basic styles, Chinese and Japanese; both are sold in covered plastic tubs, refrigerated, and usually dated to ensure freshness. The Chinese style is firm, and usually comes cut into two or four pieces—it is preferred for recipes such as stuffed bean cake. The Japanese style is softer and lighter, is used in a number of stir-fried dishes, and is especially good with hotter sauces; it sometimes comes in one big hunk, sometimes in pieces.

Brands commonly found are Wo Chong and Azumaya. Tofu should be refrigerated in water, and will keep for a few days.

BEAN CAKES, FERMENTED (Furu)

These are bean cakes that have been preserved, as are so many other Chinese foods, by fermentation. There are two kinds available: plain or with chili peppers (hot!); both come in sixteen-ounce jars. They are used in stir-fried dishes, and the plain type is also sweetened with sugar and served as an accompaniment to steamed rice. Precut into one-inch squares, they are easy to handle. Because they are naturally fermented, they will keep indefinitely in the refrigerator (as a matter of fact, they improve with age). The most common brands are Quong Hop and Wo Hop.

BEAN CURD, WET

Made from soybeans and red rice (which give it a distinctive color) and packed in brine, wet bean curd is used as a flavoring in small amounts. It is featured in Jai (Monk's Stew, a vegetarian dish traditionally served for Chinese New Year) and in a variety of stews. It comes in a can — Mee Chun and Chan Moon Kee are common brands — and will keep indefinitely in a covered jar in the refrigerator.

BEAN SAUCE

There are three kinds of bean sauce, all with quite an intense flavor: regular, hot, and sweet; all have a soybean and flour base, but little else in common, including color.

Regular is the Cantonese style, used as an additional seasoning in sauces or as a marinade, and is good in stir-fried or simmered dishes.

Hot is very hot, and should be used judiciously; ground chili peppers and extra spices add color. Commonly used in Szechuan dishes.

Sweet is only slightly so, and quite flavorful. It is sometimes used instead of hoisin sauce with Peking Duck and Mo Shu Pork, but doesn't replace hoisin sauce in cooking.

All three come in cans (Koon Chun brand is Cantonese, while Szechuan makes all three); transferred to a covered jar and refrigerated, bean sauce will last for two years.

BEAN SPROUTS

These are the sprouts of the mung bean, not to be confused with the finer-thread alfalfa sprouts. Fresh bean sprouts, barely cooked, add flavor and texture to stir-fried dishes. They should be firm and shiny (not brown or limp) and should be used soon after purchase. They may be refrigerated in a plastic bag for a day or two, but will soon lose their desirable crispness.

BEAN THREADS

Often known as cellophane noodles or Chinese vermicelli, these fine white threads are made from mung-bean starch, and are very high in protein, with a neutral flavor. They come packed in plastic bags of various sizes, and have a wide variety of uses; their *al dente* chewiness adds an interesting texture to soups and stir-fried dishes (and they pick up flavor and color from the sauce). They closely resemble rice sticks, so you should check the label.

To use, soak in cold water for five minutes, drain, dry, and cut into three-inch lengths; they cook in six minutes. Wrapped in a plastic bag, bean threads will keep indefinitely if stored in a dry place.

(Note: there is a coarser variety imported from Hong Kong or Taiwan; simply double the cooking time.)

BIRD'S NEST SOUP

Many Chinese names for foods are fanciful, but this one is not. Cliff-dwelling swallows make their nests from seaweed, binding the strands together with their saliva, which contains a substance that is glutinous and hardens quickly. The nests are harvested by hand and cleaned before using; both processes are difficult and time-consuming, so the nests are rather expensive. The resulting soup is thick and delicious and said to be very good for you.

BITTER MELON

Dark green, shaped somewhat like a zucchini, with a ridged skin, this melon contains a quinine alkaloid that gives it a bitter taste, definitely an acquired one for most people. The flavor may be mitigated by slicing the melon, salting the slices, and letting them stand for two hours, then parboiling. It will keep two to four weeks in the refrigerator. Available from late May to August.

BLACK BEANS, SALTED

Partially fermented soybeans, these come in boxes or plastic bags and are the main ingredient in the sauces for many dishes, including the delectable "lobster sauce" of Lobster Cantonese.

The word "salted" always appears prominently on the label. The beans are relatively soft, quite unlike the dried, hard beans used for soups. Used in fairly small amounts (a tablespoon or two), they should be rinsed once or twice, then mashed with a clove of garlic, which reinforces the flavor.

They will keep in a closed container for two years in the refrigerator; Yang Jiang is the best brand.

BOK CHOY

An inexpensive and popular Chinese vegetable available all year round, often referred to on Chinese restaurant menus as "Chinese greens," this is actually a member of the Swiss chard family and turns up on a lot of Italian menus as well, one of the many overlaps in the two cuisines. The entire stalk is used, including the heart. The smallest possible size is preferable, as it is more tender and has better flavor. It will keep about ten days in the refrigerator.

CHILI PASTE WITH GARLIC

You handle this stuff about the way you use nitroglycerin: with respect, and in small amounts. Composed of ground chilies, salt, soybean oil, and garlic, it is very, very hot and sharp. It is used in a number of Szechuan dishes. It comes in an eight-ounce jar (Lan Chi brand is good) and will keep in the refrigerator for two to three years.

CHINESE BROCCOLI (Gai Lon)

It looks like a scrawny version of regular broccoli, but in fact is sweet and crunchy, and the stalks are much more tender. It has fewer florets, and the leaves are larger; the whole stalk is used. It will keep in the refrigerator for seven to ten days. It is a little more expensive than regular broccoli, but as there is less waste, it is a good value.

CHINESE PARSLEY (Cilantro, Fresh Coriander)

Delicate, with bright green, full leaves, this herbaceous plant has a unique bittersweet flavor, quite distinctive. It is used to flavor steamed fish and lo mein, and is a key ingredient in Chinese Chicken Salad; it is also used as a garnish, for its eye appeal. Refrigerated, it will keep two weeks.

CHINESE SAUSAGE

Chinese sausages tend to be firmer than other types. They may be purchased individually at Chinatown sausage factories and some markets, or sold prepackaged by the pound. There are three kinds: pork (which is recommended for most purposes), beef, and duck liver (quite a strong flavor, preferred by the Chinese). The pork and beef sausages have a slightly sweet, spicy flavor, and may be steamed by themselves, or stir-fried — after steaming — with vegetables, accompanied with steamed rice. They may be refrigerated for several months, or frozen for up to a year; the price is about $4 a pound, about ten sausages.

CHOW MEIN

Quite simply, pan-fried noodles. *Chow* means "stir-fried" and *mein* means "noodles." As this is the Chinese food everybody knows best, and as it has been adapted and ruined by mass producers, fast-food restaurants, and third-rate operators, it has become a much-maligned dish, a symbol of Cantonese cliché. Nothing could be less fair; try it in Chinatown and see.

CONGEE

Either a thick rice soup or a thin rice porridge, depending on your point of view. Usually, some thin-sliced meat is added just before serving; the heat of the congee cooks it and releases its flavor. A good one-dish meal, light yet filling at the same time, and comforting on a cool day.

CORN, BABY YOUNG

Ears of immature corn, quite tender and tasty, already cooked during the canning process and slightly less sweet than the large mature version. They add interesting color and texture to stir-fry dishes. They will keep in fresh cold water in a refrigerated, covered container for about two weeks; the water should be changed every three days.

CURRY POWDER

Curry powder is a blend of a variety of spices and, used moderately, can add a pleasantly complicated flavor (and bright color) to many dishes.

Though curry originated in India, the Chinese have been trading with India for over two thousand years, and long ago adopted and adapted curry-flavored dishes.

DUCK EGGS, SALTED

Preserving by salting is an ancient process. When eggs are preserved this way, the character of the egg changes considerably: the yolk develops oils that give it a very distinctive flavor and richness; the white, when hard-boiled, is firm and very salty. There are many uses in Chinese cuisine for these eggs. They are eaten hard-boiled with rice, and the yolks are the symbolic "moon" in moon cakes. They are used raw in steamed pork cakes and are also mixed with rice and pork, wrapped in ti leaves, and cooked for hours to make joong (Chinese tamales). Local and imported salted eggs are available in Chinatown. The imported eggs may be covered with black clay, and can be mistaken for "thousand-year-old eggs," which are also enclosed in clay.

They can be found nestled in baskets in many markets, looking like small dirty potatoes. Their flavor is strong and may take some getting used to. Remove the clay under running water before cooking. The best way to try one is to hard-boil it. The price is 25 or 30¢ apiece.

DUCK EGGS, THOUSAND-YEAR-OLD

These used to be created by burying them for months, but more modern methods prevail today. The very strong, concentrated flavor remains the same, however — this is a gourmet treat for which a taste must be acquired. They need no cooking; in the preservation process, the white becomes a nearly transparent green and the yolk gray-green, the whole rather gelatinous. They are often eaten, in tiny bites, with alternate bits of preserved sweet and sour ginger, which makes a pleasant flavor combination. We recommend that you have an expert join you for your first sampling, since bad eggs turn up frequently. The price is 25 or 30¢ apiece.

EGGPLANT

Oriental eggplant has the same purple skin as the familiar pear-shaped vegetable, but is smaller — long and slender, shaped like a crookneck squash. It is more tender than the larger variety, because it is picked younger. It will keep for about two weeks in the refrigerator.

FIVE SPICE POWDER

This blend of star anise, cinnamon, fennel, cloves, and Szechuan peppercorns gives a distinctive and marvelous aroma and flavor to many dishes. Slightly sweet, with an edge of licorice, it is especially good in simmered dishes and blends well with chicken. Sold in two-ounce amounts in plastic bags, it should last indefinitely, as it is used sparingly; store in a dry place in a tightly covered container.

FUNGUS, BLACK DRIED

There are two varieties, slightly different: "wood ears" and "cloud ears." (The names are only slightly fanciful, as they are found growing on trees.) On restaurant menus, they are still named this way, but in the markets, they are usually labeled simply "Black Fungus." They don't add much flavor to dishes, but are great absorbers of sauces, and add texture to Hot and Sour Soup, Mo Shu Pork, and stir-fried dishes.

They should be soaked in hot water for about fifteen minutes; they will swell up to five times their original size. Rinse thoroughly (and discard the water), then use. Besides their other virtues, they are high in calcium, and are reputed to be effective in preventing heart problems. They will keep indefinitely at room temperature.

FUZZY MELON

Despite its forbidding appearance, this adds a nice flavor to soups and stir-fried dishes. It is green and oval, and the smaller ones (less than five inches in diameter) are more tender. Peel and use just like any other kind of summer squash. It will keep about two weeks in the refrigerator.

GARLIC

Quite a few Chinese recipes call for garlic, and markets in Chinatown sell the heads loose in bins. Since the turnover is rapid, you can be pretty sure they're the freshest in town at any given time.

GINGER ROOT

This brown, gnarled root imparts a strong, hot flavor to many dishes. It is often found in large pieces, but you may break off just as much as you need; look for a smooth skin and firmness. For cooking, break or cut off the amount you need, peel, and slice thin. There is no substitute—ginger powder is totally inadequate. Store in a cool, dry place (not in the refrigerator) for a few months. For longer storage, peel and place in a jar of white wine in the refrigerator. Change the wine (or use in cooking and replace) at least once a month.

HOISIN SAUCE

This is one of the most versatile and delicious sauces in Chinese cuisine; it is used either in cooking or as a condiment, especially with Peking Duck or Mo Shu Pork, and as the base for an excellent barbecue sauce. It is reddish-brown in color, rich and slightly sweet, made from soybeans, sugar, vinegar, fermented rice, garlic, sesame seed, chili, and spices—and the echoes of all these on your palate are subtle, but distinctive.

Because it has some of the same uses as a condiment as plum sauce (especially with pork and duck), they are sometimes confused, but they are really different; plum sauce, slightly sweeter, is not as versatile.

The most commonly found brand is Koon Chun, which comes in sixteen-ounce cans. Transferred to a jar, it will keep in the refrigerator for two or three years. (And if that happens, you should turn in your wok.)

HOT OIL

Many north Chinese restaurants have this red oil in beakers on the table, sometimes with chili pepper flakes in it, sometimes not. It is very, very hot, but good mixed with soy sauce and vinegar, in a ratio of about two parts soy sauce, two parts vinegar, one part hot oil. To make at home, heat a cup of vegetable oil for two minutes at high heat and drop in a couple of pieces of chili pepper flakes; if they sizzle, drop in 2½ teaspoons of the flakes (if they blacken, take the oil off the heat for a moment and start again). Remove from heat, let cool, and pour the oil and flakes into a bottle. Store at room temperature for a week, then use at will; it will keep for six months. Also available prepared, labeled "Chili Oil."

JICAMA

It looks like an oversized turnip, with a brown, rough skin; inside, the white flesh resembles raw potato and is crisp and moist, with a subtly sweet flavor. It may be eaten raw, used in salad, or used instead of water chestnuts in any recipe. A cut piece will keep several days in the refrigerator, stored in a plastic bag with the top left open; a whole jicama will keep several weeks.

LILY FLOWERS, DRIED

Also known as "golden needles," these slender yellow petals add color, protein, and a slightly pungent flavor to soups and stews. They should be soaked in hot water for about fifteen minutes before using. They come in four-ounce packages, but some stores repackage in one-ounce cellophane bags, which may or may not be labeled. They will keep in a dry place for two or three years.

LOBSTER SAUCE

First off, lobster sauce contains no lobster; it is the sauce that is served over lobster. But then, it's such a good sauce that the Chinese serve it over other foods, still calling it lobster sauce. The principal components are black beans, minced pork, scallions, chicken stock, and eggs.

LO MEIN

Soft noodles, briefly boiled and tossed in a hot wok with meats, sauce, seasonings, whatever.

LONG BEANS, CHINESE

These look like green beans gone wild, averaging fifteen to twenty-four inches in length. They come tied in bundles (you need not buy the whole bundle) and are used in many of the same ways as green beans — they're especially good in stir-fried dishes. They will keep well for about two weeks in the refrigerator.

LOTUS ROOT

This is a tuber of the lotus plant, which somewhat resembles a rough-skinned potato. Cut crosswise into slices, it has an attractive, lacy pattern made by the air holes within it, which enable it to float to the water's surface, flower, and reproduce (it is thus thought of as a symbol of purity and striving). Its flavor is somewhat starchy, not unlike potato but lighter, and its crisp texture enhances stir-fried dishes, stews, and especially soups — if it is used as a principal ingredient, the dish is considered a special delicacy.

Lotus root is also dried and sweetened and served as a confection at Chinese New Year, or used to sweeten tea on special occasions. It will keep in the refrigerator for two weeks.

MSG

The dreaded scourge of Chinese cooking, monosodium glutamate. It is allegedly tasteless and widely heralded as a "food enhancer," two large half-truths. In very tiny amounts it may be both, but generally it is the last refuge of unscrupulous or cheapskate cooks, who usually use too much. It causes "Chinese restaurant syndrome," characterized by dizziness, hot flashes, throbbing around the temples, and thirst. It is used much less widely now than in years past, and many restaurants proudly proclaim the premises free from the stuff, which is good. If it bothers you, always ask that your food be prepared without it — at least it's one way to keep reminding restaurants that its continuing decline is welcome.

MUSHROOMS, DRIED BLACK

While the flavor of these mushrooms is delicate, it is quite distinctive. They are somewhat expensive; the price depends on the size, and small mushrooms are much more economical for recipes calling for chopped or sliced mushrooms. They should be soaked in twice their volume of hot water for at least half an hour, or until soft, before using.

Stored in the refrigerator, tightly covered, dried black mushrooms will keep for two or three years. The price in Chinatown averages about $4.50 for a four-ounce cellophane package, but this amount is enough for several dishes.

MUSHROOMS, STRAW

Straw mushrooms are somewhat similar to our button mushrooms: they have a conical shape and a subtle flavor. They are available in sixteen-ounce cans, both peeled and unpeeled; the peeled version is much more tender. To store after opening, drain, remove mushrooms to a covered container, cover with cold water, and refrigerate. They will keep up to ten days if the water is changed every three days.

MUSTARD GREENS, CHINESE

These are available only in Chinese markets, and are actually closer to cabbage than the Western mustard greens we know. They are used for soups, and will keep in the refrigerator for about two weeks.

MUSTARD POWDER

To be used — with care — as a flavoring and as a condiment with many dishes. It is mixed into a smooth paste with equal parts cold water. There is no way to tame its hot ferocity, so small amounts should be used.

Many stores in Chinatown buy it in bulk, in twenty-pound packages, and will repackage in smaller amounts for home use. It will keep indefinitely; the average price is about $1 a pound.

NAPA CABBAGE (Chinese Cabbage, Celery Cabbage)

The best-tasting member of the cabbage family, lacking the sulphurous aroma and flavor of the coarser types. Large heads of tightly packed, pale-green, delicate leaves with sweet flavor, they are used extensively in stir-fried dishes and soups. As it is inexpensive and nutritious and there is no waste, it is an excellent value.

NUTS

Cashews, almonds, or peanuts can be bought in Chinatown groceries or health-food stores, raw, shelled, and unsalted, in eight-ounce or sixteen-ounce plastic bags. There are two methods of preparing them for a stir-fried dish: deep-fry for five minutes, drain, and add to the dish near the end of preparation; or toss in a little oil for a minute, then roast on a cookie sheet in the oven for about fifteen minutes at 325 degrees. With the second method, it's best to roast more than you need, because you will give in to temptation and nibble. The uncooked nuts will keep up to a year if refrigerated in plastic bags.

OYSTERS, DRIED

As these are very expensive, they are used sparingly, but they are essential for some dishes, such as Oyster Toss and Congee; they are also used in stews or sprinkled with ginger, steamed, and served with steamed rice as a special treat. They come in four-ounce plastic bags or eight-ounce boxes. Stored in the refrigerator, they will keep for about two years.

OYSTER SAUCE

As with so many Chinese sauces, this one doesn't taste quite as you might expect — not a lot like oysters — and if you buy a good quality brand, such as Hop Sing Lung or Lee Kum Kee, not fishy either. It is made from an extract of oysters, starch, salt, acetic acid, and some caramel coloring, which makes it dark brown. An extremely versatile primary ingredient in many sauces, it has a strong and briny flavor and, despite its origin, it goes quite well with beef and is delicious as steak sauce. It will keep up to two years in the refrigerator.

PEPPERS, DRIED RED CHILI

Frequently used in northern and Szechuan dishes, these come either whole or crushed, in 1½-ounce cellophane packages. They are, of course, extremely hot, and should be used with care. They will keep indefinitely at room temperature.

PEPPERCORNS, SZECHUAN

These have a flavor and aroma that is strikingly different from other kinds of pepper, and it's worth having some on hand to add to many dishes, or even to add to the black peppercorns in your grinder.

PLUM SAUCE

Slightly sweet, slightly spicy, warm but not hot — this yellow sauce, made from plums, sugar, vinegar, chili, and garlic, is excellent as a condiment for duck or fried squid, and is sometimes used as a dip for fried appetizers. It should be removed from the can to a jar and will keep in the refrigerator for two years.

PRESERVED RADISH

So pungent that when you open the can, the aroma will set you back a pace or two; you should rinse the pieces before using. It is preserved with chili powder, salt, and spices, and is meant to be used in fairly small doses in soups and noodle dishes, to flavor steamed pork, and in stir-frying. Sometimes also labeled "Preserved Vegetable," so check the picture on the label. One good brand is Szechuan. It should be removed from the can, placed in an airtight container, and refrigerated; it will keep up to two years.

PRESERVED VEGETABLES, TIENTSIN

This is cabbage preserved with garlic and salt, and is used to add flavor to pot stickers, pork cake, and steamed fish. It comes in a squat, brown-glazed clay pot, and there is also a spicy variety with chili added — recognizable by its orange label — that is only recommended for the adventurous. Either way, it should be used judiciously, as it is pungent. A version that comes in eight-ounce cans is also good for pot stickers and general use. It will keep in the refrigerator for up to two years, either in the original pot recovered with aluminum foil, or in a jar.

RED DATES, DRIED

Naturally sweet and very different from dark Middle Eastern-type dates, these have a flavor somewhat similar to prunes, but lighter, and are used in soups and steamed dishes. They come in eight-ounce plastic bags, but some stores repackage them in smaller amounts. Stored in a covered container in the refrigerator, they will keep for two or three years.

RICE

Of the three types of rice found in Chinese markets, **long-grain rice** is the most common, and the one you are served in restaurants. The Chinese use rice as many Americans use bread, as a bland starch to accompany other foods. They do not douse it with soy sauce, although they will place bits of food from the serving dish atop their rice bowls and eat the whole concoction together, as a way of savoring especially good sauces. Properly cooked long-grain rice is never sticky or mushy. In Chinatown, you will find it in sacks of from ten to a hundred pounds.

Short-grain rice cooks up slightly sticky, and is preferred by the Japanese. Chinese generally use it to make the rice patties for Sizzling Rice Soup and Sizzling Rice Chicken. Japanese brands available are Shira Kiku and Hinode, while Calrose is American.

Sweet rice (also known as glutinous rice) has a shiny appearance when cooked, and is used in joong (Chinese tamales), Eight Precious Pudding, and sweet rice rolls. It is too rich to eat often. The only brand available is Sho Chiku-Bai, which comes in five- and ten-pound packages, at an average price of $6 for five pounds.

All rice will keep for up to two years at room temperature in a dry place.

In many Chinese restaurants, if you have soup the waiter may not take your bowl away when he clears off the table in preparation for the next courses. The reason is that the soup bowl doubles as the rice bowl. If this strikes you as inelegant, or if you don't wish to finish whatever soup remains in the bowl, just ask for a fresh one.

RICE POWDER, GLUTINOUS

This is a form of flour made from ground raw sweet rice, and it therefore has a very glutinous quality as well as a distinctive rice flavor; it is used in many dim sum dishes. Very sticky (and somewhat difficult to work with) when moist. It comes in one-pound paper sacks, and will keep up to two years at room temperature.

RICE STICKS (Fun)

These noodles, made from rice flour, are blander than wheat noodles. Wide noodles are available fresh; the dry noodles come in two types.

Dried rice sticks are used for stir-frying (chow fun) and in soup. They are about a quarter of an inch wide, and come in one-pound bags; Lucky brand is very popular. To cook, soak them in hot water, then parboil before frying. They will keep well in their original state, up to two years at room temperature. Usually referred to as "rice noodles" on menus, sometimes merely as "fun."

Py mei fun are fine and threadlike, similar to bean threads. They are also used for stir-frying, but have a vastly different character and texture from the wider noodles and are much more interesting. They are also used for deep-frying; they puff up and become crisp in seconds. They make an interesting snack, and add texture to Cantonese Chicken Salad, Mongolian Lamb or Beef and other dishes. For deep-frying, choose the rice sticks that come in parchment paper and heat the oil to 350 degrees. Once cooked, they will keep for several days if stored in an airtight container.

RICE VINEGAR

This relatively mild vinegar is good in salad dressings and other non-Oriental foods, as well as being preferable to cider or wine vinegars for some dishes; it contributes a distinctive flavor without harshness or bite. Marukan brand comes labeled "Genuine Brewed" (green label) and "Seasoned Gourmet" (orange label), with salt, sugar, MSG, and caramel coloring added, in 12.7- and 25.4-ounce bottles; Fujita brand, also popular, comes only in 24-ounce bottles. It will keep indefinitely at room temperature.

RICE WINE

Widely used as a component in marinades for stir-fried dishes, its mild flavor is a good vehicle for various spices and condiments. Shao Hsing brand, from Taiwan, and Pagoda and Hsiang Hsueh Chiew brands, from mainland China, are the usual brands found in Chinatown, as are a variety of Japanese rice wines (sake). It needs no refrigeration.

ROASTING SALT

Roasting salt enhances flavor and gives barbecued and roasted meats (especially pork) an attractive red color. It is used in small quantities and is very inexpensive, sold loose or in small plastic packets; it will keep indefinitely in a jar in a dry place.

SALT FISH

This whole fish (packed in a plastic bag) is salted and then sun-dried, and is pungent but tasty: a little goes a long way, cut into thin strips and steamed with pork cake or steamed by itself with slivered ginger, served with steamed rice. There are many varieties, but Lee Soon Wak brand seems to have fewer bones. The unused portion should be cut into two-inch pieces and placed in a jar with vegetable oil to cover; this way it will keep for up to two years in the refrigerator.

SCALLOPS, DRIED

Shredded and used sparingly in soups, or stir-fried with eggs, these are expensive but worth it. The larger the scallop, the more expensive: the average price is about $40 a pound, but they are sold in small plastic packets, by the ounce. They will keep in a covered container in the refrigerator for two years or more.

SEAWEED

The briny flavor and purple color of dried seaweed enhance many soups. Imported from China and Japan, it comes in thin sheets, about two ounces worth, in cellophane packages, sometimes also labeled "Dried Laver," sometimes not labeled at all. It will keep indefinitely in a dry place at room temperature.

SESAME OIL

Pressed from sesame seeds, this oil has a delightful and quite
distinctive flavor that could be overpowering unless used
sparingly. It is used both as a condiment and a seasoning in many
dishes, especially in the Mandarin and Szechuan cuisines.
Common brands are Lucky and Sona Food Company, in six-ounce
and sixteen-ounce bottles. Sesame oil should be refrigerated after
opening; it will keep over two years if properly stored. When
chilled, it solidifies slightly, but can be used immediately for
cooking. If you are using it as a condiment, pour out only the
amount needed and let stand at room temperature before using.
Non-Oriental sesame oils, found in supermarkets, are very
different; they are general cooking oils, not flavoring agents.

SESAME SEEDS

White sesame seeds are used often in Chinese cooking, imparting
both flavor and texture to many dishes. The most economical way
to purchase them is in bulk from a Chinese market (and the least
economical way is from health-food stores). Black sesame seeds
are used less often, but are available in some stores. Sesame seeds
will keep for a few months at room temperature; the average price
is about 50¢ for four ounces.

SESAME SEED PASTE

Made from ground sesame seeds and soybean oil, this has a very
concentrated nutty flavor. It is used as a flavoring for sauces,
rather than in cooking. Lan Chi brand is the best. Sesame seed
paste will keep two years in a jar in the refrigerator.

SNOW PEAS (Chinese Pea Pods)

One of the choicest of Chinese vegetables, prized for its flavor,
crisp texture, and colorful eye appeal. The flatter the pod, the
younger and better it is. Available year round, but twice as expensive in winter, they will keep about two weeks in the refrigerator,
in a paper bag.

SOY SAUCE

Soy sauce is the closest thing to an all-purpose sauce in the Orient. It is used as a condiment, a marinade, and a component of many dishes that feature other sauces. It is generally notable for its saltiness, but several Japanese brands, widely available, are fairly bland, and may suit more people's preference.

Thin soy sauce, also called "light" soy sauce, is made from fermented soybean extract, wheat flour, salt, and water. It has a thin consistency and a slightly lighter color, and is more salty than the dark sauce.

Dark soy sauce, also sometimes called "black" soy sauce, contains sugar or molasses in addition to the other ingredients, has a thicker consistency, less saltiness, and more flavor than thin soy sauce.

Soy sauce will keep well for many months at room temperature after opening, or for two or more years in the refrigerator. The reliable brands are Pearl River Bridge (from mainland China), and Koon Chun and Golden Label (from Hong Kong). Pearl River Bridge bottles both varieties in identical bottles, with almost identical labels; their thin sauce is labeled "Superior Soy," while their dark sauce is labeled "Soy, Superior Sauce."

SHARK'S FIN

Aside from being delicious, this is thought to have great restorative powers (probably true, as it's very high in protein). Shavings of shark's fin are simmered with other flavorings in chicken stock to make a rich broth. It is expensive, and worth it. Available whole or as shavings in many stores.

SHRIMP, DRIED

These are usually the small bay shrimp, and the drying process concentrates the flavor so that a small amount added to a dish is almost like adding an extra spice or condiment. Sold in cellophane packages, they should be rinsed and soaked before using. Relatively expensive, but worth it, they will keep well in a covered container in the refrigerator for up to two years.

SQUID, DRIED

Very different in taste and texture from fresh squid, and used to add flavor to various dishes—it's subtle, but very interesting. Rinse, soak, and cut into strips before adding. Sold in eight-ounce cellophane packets, it will keep at room temperature for up to one year.

STAR ANISE

One of the elements of five spice powder, this is a star-shaped seed pod with a strong licorice flavor, used mainly in stews and very aromatic. It is sold in two-ounce plastic bags. Usually the pods break up from the star, so remember that eight pods make one star. It will keep indefinitely in a closed container in a dry place.

SUBGUM

A mixture of meats or vegetables; the term most commonly refers to noodle dishes that feature more than one kind of meat.

TANGERINE PEEL, DRIED

The peel of tangerines, tangelos, or Mandarin oranges, preserved by drying. It is used for extra flavor in soups, stews, and steamed fish. Sold in one-ounce cellophane packets and sometimes simply labeled "Orange Peel," it will keep indefinitely in a cool, dry place.

TAPIOCA STARCH (Tapioca Powder)

A smooth white powder resembling cornstarch, used to thicken sauces; it may be used instead of cornstarch, but makes a thicker sauce and should be used with care. It is also used in some dim sum dishes.

TARO ROOT

Taro root resembles a beet, but tastes more like a yam (it is used for poi in Hawaii). It has a wide variety of uses in Chinese cooking: mashed for deep-fried taro root dumplings (a dim sum dish); stewed with pork; boiled and served much like potato; and diced and mixed with Chinese sausage, mushrooms, dried shrimp, and rice flour to make a steamed pudding. Another delicious dish, served in some restaurants, consists of taro root slivers molded into a basket, deep-fried, then filled with meat and vegetables — a delightful contrast of tastes and textures. Taro root will keep in the refrigerator for a month.

WATER CHESTNUT POWDER (Water Chestnut Starch)

Used mostly in batters for deep-frying, this is grainier than corn-starch. It comes in eight-ounce boxes and the brands most commonly seen are Companion and Chi Kong. It will keep indefinitely at room temperature in a dry place.

WATER CHESTNUTS, FRESH

There is a world of difference between these and the bland canned versions, which lose a lot of flavor and texture in the canning process. Fresh water chestnuts are crisp and have a slightly sweet taste, similar to coconut, but a lot less trouble to get at. The flavor they add to a dish is well worth the time taken to peel them, and the job is made easier by a little discreet snacking as you go. Peeled, immersed in water, and refrigerated, they will retain flavor and texture for two days; unpeeled and dry, for two weeks.

WINTER MELON

This large green member of the squash family has a variety of
uses, and one of the best is soup. Its flavor is fairly bland, so the
other soup ingredients are important. The economy version is just
pieces of melon simmered with other ingredients; in the spectacular version, the soup is served in the shell, which is quite
large. If you are planning a banquet, you should order this in
advance (it takes hours to cook) to be sure of getting the latter.

Tips on Tea
(and other beverages)

TEA

Sometimes there seem to be as many theories about the origin of tea as there are varieties of the beverage. Forgive us for saying this, but most of them don't hold water. Certainly none give any credit to the ingenuity of the Chinese people, who have not only found ways to utilize as food almost everything that grows, but also to make it taste good.

The tea plant is a member of the family Theceae, the tea family (*Camillia sinensis*), a fairly hardy shrub that grows best in high altitudes such as those found in China, Japan, and India. Tea was used in China more than two thousand years ago, mainly as a curative, refreshing, and medicinal beverage, and was first cultivated for wider use about fourteen hundred years ago. Its popularity seems to have been immediate, and it spread throughout Asia and eventually around the world.

Throughout its history, people have attempted to "improve" the flavor of tea by adding other flavorings. Long ago, the Chinese added onions and salt to the infusion; in many Arab countries, mint is added; the British add milk or lemon and sugar; New Englanders many years ago added fruits and spices (and rum, sometimes); and every country, at one time or another, has felt compelled to add flower petals. With the exception of the latter, most of these additions produce dubious beverages; they traduce, rather than enhance, the flavor of the tea.

What is most amazing about tea is that hundreds of kinds of it derive from the same species; its characteristics vary according to growing conditions such as soil, altitude, and climate, of course, and these are crucial factors in its ultimate quality. Another important factor is the time it is picked—a tea shrub may be harvested several times annually, and the first picks are the best, because then the leaves are tender and full of flavorful oils but still low in tannins, which can make tea bitter.

Basically, there are three classifications of tea, with many variations within each: green tea, black tea, and oolong. More than one type may even come from the same plant, as these types are created by different fermentations, or the lack of them.

In wine, cheese, and bread, fermentation begins as a result of the action of yeasts. For tea, it is the process of oxidation—exposure to air and then heat—that causes a chemical change in the oils.

Green tea is unfermented, only lightly handled in the processing, and frequently made from young, tender small leaves. When dry, the small leaves are gray-green in color, and were thought by early traders to resemble gunpowder, one of the names green tea is still known by today (it was also sometimes adulterated with gunpowder in eighteenth-century England — to give it a bang?). The liquid is golden, the flavor and aroma subtle and refreshing. It goes best with lighter, blander foods. Varieties are Dragon Well, Sui Sen, Imperial Gunpowder (or other variations of gunpowder), and Young Hyson. Chrysanthemum tea, slightly bittersweet, has a green-tea base.

Oolong is semifermented, with brownish-black leaves that produce a yellowish tea of moderate aroma and flavor. Basically a good all-purpose tea, it falls somewhere between green and black in flavor intensity, though it usually lacks the unusual character found in the other two types. Grown mostly in Taiwan (thus the familiar Formosa oolong), and in some places on the mainland, it goes well with a wide variety of foods. Jasmine tea is often made with oolong, scented with jasmine flowers.

Black tea is fully fermented and has a wide variety of flavors and uses. The leaves are indeed black, and the liquid is a rich reddish-brown. Flavored teas, such as Lichee, and smoked teas, such as Lapsang Souchong, are also in this category. Some notable varieties are Keemun (from Taiwan, also known as Winey Keemun, for its rich red color), Po Nay, Yunnan Black, and Rare Mandarin. Black tea is a good accompaniment to deep-fried or strong-flavored foods, and a good breakfast drink.

Two unusual presentations of tea can be found in Chinatown stores: Lok On, a semifermented tea a little stronger than oolong, comes wrapped in broad *ti* leaves and packed in a straw basket — the brand is Hung Chong Tai, and it's delicious. You can also get Po Nay tea pressed into round bricks — just break off what you need to brew. Long ago in China, tea was used as currency in this manner, embossed with the seal of whatever emperor was running things; it was also a convenient way of shipping tea long distances overland (there is a blended black tea called Russian Caravan, supposedly based on the czar's favorites). These bricks are plain, and the liquid tea is strong and earthy.

Any grocery store or market in Chinatown can be counted on to have a good selection of teas, often packaged in attractive tea caddies (canisters); many also have packs of several kinds of teas, a good way to sample the different varieties.

You may also see, in quite a few stores that carry pottery and china, cups with covers. In Chinese homes, tea is often brewed right in the cup for honored guests; these cups also make sense for those who only want a small amount of tea (the cup can be refilled with boiling water—the Chinese say that the second cup is better than the first).

Aside from the considerable virtues of its flavor, tea has a number of other attributes. Taken as is, as the Chinese do, it contains no calories or carbohydrates. China teas are also slightly lower in caffeine than other kinds of tea, and only contain about one-third the amount of caffeine per cup as the same amount of coffee ("breakfast teas" are usually from India—and are so-called because you get more of a jolt from them).

Tea is also quite economical. On the average, a pound of tea will yield over two hundred cups, much more than a pound of coffee.

Some people make a lot of fuss about equipment and techniques for brewing tea; such people will always be with us. Really, there are only a few simple principles to keep in mind to get the most and best pleasure and flavor out of it.

First, a good solid teapot is essential, preferably of thick chinaware; glass and metal lose heat too rapidly.

Use one teaspoon of tea leaves to each quart of water. People in the tea business tell you to use more; so would we, if we were in the tea business. This amount gives you perfect color and flavor. By the way, never boil tea, as it concentrates the brew and brings out the tannins, making it bitter.

While the water is coming to the boil, warm the teapot by adding hot water (just running hot water from the faucet is fine), pouring it out, and bringing it close to the kettle. "Take the teapot to the kettle, not the kettle to the teapot," says the sage.

Pour the boiling water over the leaves. Some people pour a few ounces of water over them, return the kettle to the fire for a minute, and then fill the teapot with the remainder of the boiling water, on the theory that the first pour "opens up" the flavor quicker. We tried it both ways in glass containers to observe the transformation, and it doesn't seem to make any difference.

Allow the tea to steep for at least five minutes before serving.

If you are going to be drinking the tea over a period of short time, a tea cozy isn't a bad idea, and many Chinatown shops sell padded baskets that will keep the pot warm. A better idea may be to pour the tea into a thermos (Camel brand, from Hong Kong, is excellent), where it will stay hot for hours.

Some people don't like to make or drink loose tea because of the bits of tea leaves that come out when they fill a cup. Our friend, the estimable Preston Wong, showed us how to overcome this: When the tea is ready for pouring, simply pick up the pot and rock it gently but briskly from side to side for a moment. The tea leaves (most of them, anyway) will sink to the bottom and the tea will be clear when poured.

BEER

Beer is a popular drink with the Chinese, though not necessarily as an accompaniment to food. It would be appropriate with a meal composed of all-Szechuan food, to bank the fires (though hot tea works just as well), or to begin a meal, along with appetizers such as egg rolls, fried won ton, deep-fried chicken wings, and the like. On the other hand, it would clash with and overwhelm a number of Cantonese and Mandarin dishes, wiping out their subtle flavors.

The most widely available Chinese beer is Tsingtao, a light, dry Pilsener-type beer, not much different from most American beers; it has just a bit more maltiness. Like many imported beers, it is not found in a number of restaurants in Chinatown, since it is simply not worth the extra money. Politics may also sometimes be a factor, as it is brewed in the People's Republic of China.

A number of Japanese beers are frequently available, also in the light, dry Pilsner style; they are a little maltier and more flavorful than American beers, and are more reasonable in price than other imports. Kirin and Sapporo are the most popular brands. Both also produce "black beer" (which is merely dark), slightly sweet and full-bodied, very pleasant-tasting. Light and dark versions, in a similar vein, sometimes turn up from San Miguel, a brewery in the Philippines.

Beer has been brewed in Asia for not much more than one hundred years; the Germans started it in China, while the Americans began it in Japan.

WINE

The subject of Chinese food and wine fascinates wine buffs, but then, they're easily fascinated by food-and-wine questions. In a Western dinner, with a stately procession of different courses, with separate meat and vegetable dishes, and with the emphasis in each course on that particular meat or fowl or fish, wine has an essential place as an accompaniment.

On the other hand, the Chinese meal is a mélange of dishes served almost at once and featuring fish, fowl, and meat sometimes at the same sitting, with an abundance of vegetables mixed in and with delicate sauces, so that it's ridiculous to try "correct" matchups. Even in a banquet setting, where course follows course, it can be more fatiguing than enjoyable. In Chinese banquets, most drinks are consumed between courses, however, and here wine, with its ability to clear and refresh the palate, is appropriate.

If you have any control over the menu for a banquet, you might try serving several white-meat courses in sequence with white wines, and then some red wines with later meat courses if the sauces aren't too pungent or hot. Or, if there are just a few people dining lightly, a carafe of house white wine would be a good choice; light white wine generally matches light foods well.

To some extent, the matter is moot, simply because most restaurants in Chinatown don't have much of a wine list. Many restaurants will allow you to bring in your own wine, though you may have to drink it out of a water glass.

The Restaurants
of Chinatown

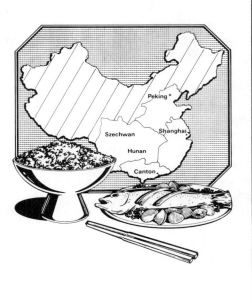

When this book was begun, there were, by actual on-foot count, ninety-three restaurants within the borders of Chinatown; when it was ended, there were ninety-five. As you read this, that number has probably changed again.

As we noted previously, the predominant flavor of Chinatown is Cantonese, but there have been significant inroads by other regions over the years, and many menus are rather eclectic today, with smatterings and borrowings from all over the place; any Cantonese place has, for example, at least a few hot northern-style dishes on the menu, as well as Mandarin dishes such as pot stickers, and eastern China dishes like paper-wrapped chicken, pressed duck, and cold noodles. In the end it matters less that West Lake Beef Soup originated in Hangchow than that it be delicious now on Powell Street, where no restaurants feature the cuisine of the province in question.

With that in mind, we have concentrated more on what is unique, different, and good than on what might be comfortingly familiar, "correct," safe and tidy, while not straying into exotica like fish bellies, sea cucumbers, and various kinds of jellyfish — they're not bad, but they're not delicious, either.

We've also not presented overcrowded places like Hunan, Sam Wo's (the Caffé Sport of Chinatown, thanks to the fearsome Edsel Ford Fong), Yuet Lee, and restaurants that feature color photos of cliché dishes in the window. We have chosen a cross-section of dishes, restaurants, styles, and price ranges — from humble noodle shops to "tablecloth" places, with plenty in between — that encapsulates the considerable and delightful choices of Chinatown.

A good rule of thumb when ordering in a Chinese restaurant: one dish per person, plus soup and rice. For larger groups, say eight or ten people, ask for a double order of each. For maximum enjoyment, strive for balance, that is to say, a variety of foods — poultry, seafood, meat, vegetables, different sauces, and different degrees of hotness or spiciness; the contrasts make for the balance.

On the front of menus in Chinatown will often be found a Chinese menu, usually one sheet, listing in Chinese characters a variety of dishes (in some restaurants, there are two entirely separate menus). There is no discrimination or snobbishness involved here, just a classically logical Chinese response to the fact that they serve two different clienteles, one of which is not noted for being daring about "exotic" foods. Chinese cuisine is predicated on fresh food and no waste, so it doesn't make sense to list — and stock — items they can't anticipate a demand for. Additionally, the Chinese menu is a great place for highly seasonal items, or something that simply looked good at the market that morning.

The result is a classic dilemma that sometimes seems insurmountable — the Chinese folks at the next table are eating more appetizing-looking food than you are. Calvin Trillin tells the story of a friend of his who carried around a card on which was written in Chinese characters, "Please bring me some of what that man at the next table is having." The usual riposte was, of course, "You no like." We have tried to help by indicating the names of some dishes listed only on the Chinese menu. Ordering this way, we have found that waiters are very good about not telling us we no like; in fact, they will usually suggest other dishes once they know you're really interested, and there are a lot worse things than putting yourself in their hands altogether if you're hitting it off.

Our criteria for prices is: under five dollars per person for a full meal, inexpensive; five to eight dollars, moderate; anything over, expensive. You can eat better and cheaper in Chinatown than in most other areas of San Francisco, and we hope you will. We have noted the places that serve beer, wine, and other beverages.

ASIA GARDEN

772 Pacific Avenue (near Stockton)
398-5112
Cuisine: Cantonese and dim sum
Price range: Moderate
Hours: 9–3 daily for dim sum, 5–10 daily for dinner
Credit cards: (dinner only) American Express, Visa
Full bar

During the day, Asia Garden is a classic dim sum restaurant, large and noisy and bustling—and very good. In the evening, the upstairs-balcony dining areas are closed up, and the lower floor is transformed into a pleasant, quiet dining room, with tablecloths, candles, and attractive wooden screens that hem the room into something like intimacy.

Winter Melon Soup comes in a rich and complex version here, containing chicken stock and meat, mushrooms, bamboo shoots, and peas, with large chunks of the delicately flavored winter melon.

Beef with Tender Greens is a great success; the chunks of beef are good meat marinated in a mix of seasonings and then stir-fried in a thick, tasty, slightly sweet sauce. *Sweet and Sour Pork Chops* are far beyond the usual candy-flavored version; thin strips are dipped in a light batter and then deep-fried and served coated with a sauce containing honey and vinegar and other seasonings.

Among the unusual dishes found here is *Raw Fish Salad,* which requires one-day advance notice. It serves ten people and contains raw fish, pickled ginger, scallions, various vegetables, shredded green onions, daikon radish, parsley, chopped roasted peanuts, sesame seeds, deep-fried won ton skins and rice sticks, all bathed in a wonderful mix of spices. This dish is especially good in the winter, as the fish used in winter is blackfish (seen swimming in tanks in the fish markets), which has a sweet and delicate flavor.

Crab is also a great dish here, when in season. It is sautéed in the shell with either curry, black bean, or ginger and green onion sauce. It is a little messy, but well worth it.

Asia Garden is very popular on weekends for dinner because of good food and good value; things are a little easier during the week, when reservations are not necessary.

BOW HON

850 Grant Avenue (between Clay and Washington)
362-0601
Cuisine: Cantonese
Price range: Moderate
Hours: 9—9, closed Thursday
No credit cards
Beer only

This looks like a hole-in-the-wall place and is usually full, but
there is an overflow dining room upstairs. Bow Hon is as bare and
plain as they come, but the staff is helpful and friendly, and the
cooks are more imaginative than the menu writer.

A specialty of the house is clay-pot dishes. One rarity is *Monk's
Stew (Jai),* a vegetarian stew of bean curd, seaweed, peas,
mushrooms, golden needles, bamboo shoots, and, it seems,
whatever else is on the market or the chef's mind that day. It's a
little monotonous for one, but would be a good component in a
meal for four or more. *Sizzling Chicken in Gravy* and *Bean Cake
with Assorted Meats* are our clay-pot favorites.

Combination rice plates are good, inexpensive one-dish meals.
Spareribs with Soybean Sauce, Tender Greens with Shrimp, and *Sam See
with Oyster Sauce* (shredded barbecued pork, chicken, bamboo
shoots, yellow onion, and bean sprouts) are recommended.

On the Chinese menu, try *Mandarin Spareribs,* meaty ones
dipped in batter, deep-fried, and served with a light sweet-sour
sauce containing Chinese pickled vegetables, quite a change from
the usual. Another winner is *King Tu Beef with Chinese Greens:*
marinated beef chunks cooked in sweet-spicy hoisin sauce, over
lightly sautéed hearts of bok choy; the sauce is thick and rich, the
greens crisp and refreshing, the whole a perfect balance.

BRANDY HO'S

217 Columbus (at Pacific)
788-7527
Cuisine: Hunanese
Price range: Moderate
Hours: Sun—Thurs 11:30—9:30, Fri—Sat 11:30—11
Credit cards: MasterCard, Visa
Beer and wine

This place is a Chinese version of the North Beach joints where you can sit at the counter and watch the food being cooked, except that here it's done in large woks. It's an attractive room with a high ceiling that gives it an airy feel, enhanced by tasseled lanterns, plants, and paintings and masks on the walls. Brandy is the dapper gentleman responsible for all this, and his brother presides over the woks. They do not believe in holding back on spices, especially ginger and garlic.

You can make a good start with *Onion Cakes,* thin wheat-flour pancakes flavored by green onion; try *Fried Dumplings with Special Sauce,* "little purse" dumplings filled with coarsely ground pork, fresh ginger, garlic, and vegetables — a unique version; *Julienne Eggplant Salad* is steamed eggplant strips in a dressing of hot oil, vinegar, parsley, and garlic — the temperature is cool, the sauce hot.

Now you're ready to eat. Hunanese smoked specialties are made on the premises, and worth trying — they're done over hard wood in the old-fashioned way, to develop the strong smoky flavor so popular in Hunan province. Ham, chicken, duck, and bacon are featured.

Hot and Sour Chicken is another unique dish: diced chicken sautéed with bell pepper, young bamboo shoots, minced ginger and garlic, in a sweet-hot-sour sauce. *Deep-fried Shredded Pork with Vegetables and Hot Bean Sauce* is just what it says, and quite good. *Brandy's Dinner* is stir-fried beef, shrimp, and scallops, slightly hot, while *Brandy Ho's Spareribs* are braised in a honey-and-vinegar sauce and coated with sesame seeds. Brandy only puts his name on dishes he's especially proud of, so let that be your guide.

One other thing he's proud enough about to put up on the wall: absolutely no MSG used here.

CANTON TEA HOUSE

1108 Stockton Street (between Jackson and Pacific)
982-1030
Cuisine: Cantonese and dim sum
Price range: Moderate
Hours: 7:30 A.M.–9:30 P.M. daily
       (dim sum from 7:30 A.M.–3 P.M. daily)
No credit cards
Beer only

By day, this large restaurant is crowded and bustling, a tribute to
its excellent dim sum as well as other light dishes. At dinner, the
pace and crowds are easier. The menu is large and varied, the food
is quite good, and the large portions make it a bargain.

Two soups are outstanding: *Corn Soup with Chicken Slices*
contains creamed corn, chicken, egg drop, and bamboo shoots in
chicken stock, very rich and filling; *Bird's Nest Soup with Crab* is a
fine example of this dish, also rich.

A specialty we highly recommend is *Canton Special Chicken,*
unique and delicious. Pieces of boneless chicken are marinated in
a dark, thin sauce, then stir-fried with black mushrooms, Chinese
greens, and thin slices of carrots. This mixture is poured over
crisp deep-fried chicken wings.

Braised Whole Rock Cod is actually deep-fried and comes in
several sauces; it is also available as cut-up fillets, listed as *Boneless
Rock Cod.* A terrific version comes in black bean sauce; a quite
unusual one features sweet and sour sauce, with chunks of pineapple, green pepper, and onion — somehow it works.

Good menu-balancers with these would be *Sautéed Scallops,*
which come with the best vegetables of the day, and *Sirloin Cubes
with Tender Greens,* good beef marinated in a light sauce, then
stir-fried with bok choy. There are also a couple of good crab
dishes in season, well worth asking about.

CELADON

881 Clay Street (between Grant and Stockton)
982-1168
Cuisine: Cantonese, Mandarin, and dim sum
Price range: Moderate to expensive
Hours: Lunch Mon–Sat 11:30–2:30; dinner 5–11 daily
      (dim sum 9 A.M.–3 P.M. daily)
All major credit cards
Full bar

Celadon is a beautiful restaurant that wears its formality lightly. An attractive bar area is at ground level to one side as you enter, and the dining room is up a short flight of steps to the right, under a large and shimmering chandelier. The room is graced with beautiful paintings and painted screens; the table settings are formal and the noise level is subdued.

All this usually adds up to a less-than-satisfying Chinese restaurant experience, but rest assured, the kitchen here is firmly on your side.

For one thing, the beef is high quality and generously portioned, so we can recommend all the selections; especially good is *Beef with Spicy Tea Sauce* and *Beef with Snow Peas* (which here are barely cooked—quite tasty and crisp).

Celadon Spareribs are also good quality and very meaty, and the sauce that coats them is light, sweet, and spicy—definitely not the usual. Also different and delicious are the *Sliced Chicken with Walnut Paste* and *Whole Deep-fried Squab*.

The seafood list is extensive, and includes fish, scallops, prawns, and crab; given the talent for sauces here, it's hard to see where you could go wrong with any of them, though we lean to prawns or lobster (at a very reasonable price) in black bean sauce.

There are a number of oyster dishes here that are worth trying—including deep-fried oysters with ginger and green onion, and *Minced Dried Oysters Wrapped in Lettuce*. Dried oysters are notably strong, but the other flavorings minced into this dish give it a whole that is greater than the sum of its parts.

DING HO

836 Washington Street (between Grant and Stockton)
986-2252
Cuisine: Cantonese
Price range: Moderate
Hours: 11:30–10 daily
No credit cards

Ding Ho is very much the prototypical Chinese restaurant that prevails all over America: fake wood paneling on the walls, plain tables and chairs, mirrors as the major decorative touches, not much English spoken, small. One look at the menu, however, and you know you're not in Cleveland.

For one thing, eight different preparations of bean curd are offered, in intriguing combinations of meat, vegetables, and spices; we leave the choice to your sense of adventure. There are also a number of seasonal crab and fish dishes worth inquiring about.

Fifteen different rice plates are offered, each a hearty combination of meat, fish, or poultry and vegetables over a mound of steamed rice, an inexpensive and satisfying meal. We recommend *Beef with Tomato, Chicken with Black Mushrooms, Beef with Tender Greens, Ginger and Green Onion Beef, Scrambled Egg with Shrimp,* and *Oyster Sauce Sum See* (chicken, shrimp, and bamboo shoots).

Spicy Sand Dabs are unique and special. The fish are boned, very lightly cooked with a delicately gingered sauce with snow peas, scallions, and carrots; then served, in brightly multicolored glory, on a thin carpet of their fried bones and tails—odd, but pretty.

We can also recommend *Sautéed Clams with Black Bean Sauce, Szechuan Shrimp* (the sauce is moderately hot and red), and *Pepper and Black Bean Chicken,* a jazzy variation of the usual black bean rendition.

FAR EAST CAFE

631 Grant Avenue (between California and Sacramento)
982-3245
Cuisine: Cantonese
Price range: Moderate
Hours: Mon—Fri 11:30—10, Sat—Sun noon—10
All major credit cards
Full bar

The Far East first opened in 1920, and is now managed by the third generation of the same family; they have well preserved its antiquarian charms. Large and ornate antique chandeliers hang from the high ceilings of the downstairs dining room, and part of the space is divided by high partitions into curtained booths—the total effect is quite theatrical.

The food is no letdown, though the menu is plain and even cryptic. The *Paper-wrapped Chicken* is an excellent version, tender boneless pieces marinated in seasoning, wrapped in parchment paper, and deep-fried; the result is moist and flavorful, slightly messy, and fun. *Winter Melon Soup* is also well prepared: diced melon is combined with chicken, bamboo shoots, water chestnuts, and rich broth.

Prawns with Black Bean Sauce are only lightly garlicked and combined with fresh green peppers and yellow onions; the portion is generous. *Subgum Vegetables* feature a good hunk of the garden: baby ears of corn, carrots, celery, Chinese greens, straw mushrooms, black mushrooms, water chestnuts, bamboo shoots, and whatever else the chef feels it needs to make it credible. This is a perfect meal-balancer; the sauce is very light, the vegetables crisp and undercooked. *Peking Beef* features a hotter sauce, and tops a pile of greens. *Pressed Mandarin Duck* is available, a better version than the usual.

FORTUNE RESTAURANT

675 Broadway (between Grant and Stockton)
421-8130
Cuisine: Chiu Chow
Price range: Moderate
Hours: 10 A.M.–midnight daily
Credit cards: MasterCard, Visa
Beer and wine

Chiu Chow (pronounced Chow Joe) cooking is the latest distinct culinary style to arrive in San Francisco, and there are two such places serving it in Chinatown (the other is the Golden Pagoda). The Chiu Chow district is in Kwangtung province, north of Canton, where a river delta meets the sea and raw ingredients are diverse. The main influence on this cuisine, though, is the fact that when many of the people fled China during one of its periodic upheavals more than one hundred years ago, they resettled in Southeast Asia; now, their cooking has evolved, generally, into a quite spicy and frequently hot bias, but with very light sauces (including fish sauces), different from Szechuan and other hot northern styles.

The Fortune opened early in 1982, and was an immediate success. We visited it several times right after it opened, and observed the same man there every day. It turned out that he'd been in opening day and had the *Shark's Fin Soup,* and liked it so much that he came back again and again for it! In fact, it is one of the specialties of Chiu Chow cuisine, and we second his opinion; four varieties are served here and all are excellent; the *Shark's Fin in Chicken Broth* is especially good. (It's best to order one day in advance, to make sure they don't run out.)

There are six fish dishes, all recommended — the owner is quite proud of their freshness and variety. Bream is featured in several versions, notably pan-fried; it's good but a little expensive, as it's a small fish. *Steamed Fish with Black Bean Sauce,* made with rock cod, is very tasty.

Spiced and Peppered Chicken is small pieces of chicken fried in a spicy but very light sauce, which has a complex, intriguing flavor. *Hot and Spicy Beef Noodles* features wide rice noodles stir-fried and coated with a spicy sauce with a cumulative hot punch to it. *Assorted Seafood in a Pot* is an amalgamation of oysters, prawns, squid, and fish cooked in chicken broth, served quite hot in a casserole.

Two dishes would go well as appetizers or parts of a large meal. *Saday Beef* is thin slices of meat on skewers, accompanied with a hot pepper-peanut sauce, reflecting an Indonesian influence; and *Fried Fish Cake* is actually minced fish and water chestnuts wrapped in a bean-curd skin, deep-fried, and served with a light sweet-sour sauce. It looks like an odd sausage cut into bite-size slices, and it's delicious.

GOLDEN DRAGON NOODLE SHOP

833 Washington Street (corner of Waverly)
398-4550
Cuisine: Cantonese
Price range: Inexpensive
Hours: 7 A.M. – 1 A.M. daily
No credit cards

This is a small, quick-service place with a clientele almost exclusively Chinese. It is usually crowded and serves plain but good food.

Won Ton in Supreme Soup has the best won ton in town — lots of filling and good flavor. *Won Ton and Noodle Soup* is the same, with noodles added; you may also order barbecued pork or roast duck as garnish, at a slight extra cost.

The congee here is also quite good, listed on the menu as *Rice Soup.* This is the largest selection in Chinatown, and we recommend *Beef, Pork Meatball, Chicken, Sliced Fish and Meatball, Abalone and Dicked Chicken,* and *Sampan,* which is the deluxe version featuring chicken, shrimp, dried squid, pork, and meat-balls, with a garnish of deep-fried peanuts.

The noodles here are good, with quite a selection of chow mein, lo mein, and chow fun; and there are also a number of rice plates.

This is the place for good, fast food — if you can get in. They also do a good business in take-outs.

GOLDEN PAGODA

960 Grant Avenue (between Washington and Jackson)
397-1411
Cuisine: Chiu Chow
Price range: Moderate
Hours: 11–10 daily
No credit cards

The Golden Pagoda is a small walk-up overlooking the corner of Grant and Jackson, plain as a mud fence, but delightful. The kitchen is in full view, and the cooks are great performers.

There are quite a few notable things to try here, and it's worth repeat visits. Start with *Deep-fried Shrimp Roll* (Chinese menu only), a mixture of minced shrimp, pork, water chestnuts, green onion, and seasonings wrapped in a sheet of dried bean curd and deep-fried, served with plum sauce on the side. *Seaweed and Fish Ball Soup* (Chinese menu only) is quite mild and tasty; freshly made fish balls are somewhat similar to firm tofu, with a light fish flavor — very refreshing.

Chiu Chow Chicken is also only on the Chinese menu: odd-shaped pieces of chicken well sautéed (firmly cooked and crisp) in an indefinable, complex sauce. *Chiu Chow-Style Soy Sauce Duck* is cold duck that has been stewed in seasoned soy sauce and chopped into chunks, with the bones still in, like spareribs; the salty-smoky flavor makes gnawing worthwhile. *Stir-fried Beef with Rice Noodles* is unique. The noodles are the dried rice sticks that must be boiled before using, and the sauce is a bit spicy-hot. On the English menu, it is listed as a soup, so be sure to request it "stir-fried" instead. It is usually served with Chinese broccoli.

There are seven different versions of *Shark's Fin Soup* on the menu, and it is the family's pride and joy; try the braised style or the version with crab meat.

THE GOLDEN PAVILION

800 Sacramento Street (at Grant)
392-2334
Cuisine: Cantonese, Mandarin, Szechuan, dim sum (lunch only)
Price range: Expensive
Hours: Lunch 11–2:30 daily;
       dinner Mon–Fri 5:30–10, Sat–Sun 5:30–11
All major credit cards
Full bar

The Golden Pavilion is an attractive, decorous, good-sized place overlooking Grant Avenue, the kind of place that purists think of as a tourist trap and not the "real" Chinatown (whatever that is). To be sure, the menu is somewhat middle of the road; the food is much better at lunch, for some reason; the dinner-time formality takes a lot of the fun out of the experience; and one featured dish wins the prize as the most peculiar we have encountered: *Deepfried Squid in Sweet and Sour Sauce,* proudly cited on the menu as found only here (for which, thank God).

Yet it is worth a visit. There is a choice of six kinds of tea, for one thing, including the fairly rare Iron Kuan Yin, a black tea. Two Szechuan dishes are done well: *Szechuan Prawns,* tossed in herbs and hot spices, and *Szechuan Pepper Chicken,* which also includes peppers, peanuts, bamboo shoots, and mushrooms. Also, *Silver and Gold Noodles* is marvelous — the "silver" is fresh rice noodles, and the "gold" is pan-fried wheat noodles tossed together with barbecued pork, black mushrooms, bamboo shoots, and snow peas.

Something unique is *Golden Pavilion Cream Soufflé,* a whippedtogether wet fluff of ham and abalone and unidentifiable bits suspended in egg white and cream, with crisp puffed rice sticks here and there to surprise and delight you.

GOLDEN PHOENIX

729 Washington Street (between Kearny and Grant)
362-5475
Cuisine: Cantonese
Price range: Moderate
Hours: Mon–Fri 11:30–10:30, Sat–Sun 4–10:30
Credit cards: MasterCard, Visa
Full bar

The Golden Phoenix is quite attractive, with tan and silver wall-paper featuring its namesake, Chinese lanterns with red tassels, white tablecloths, and a wall-length mirror that makes the place seem larger.

The menu features a good selection of Cantonese dishes and the kitchen executes them well. *Shrimp with Lobster Sauce* is out-standing, with one of the best versions of this sauce we've had — thick, rich, and balanced. *Beef Under Snow* is strips of beef, bamboo shoots, and mixed vegetables topped with deep-fried rice sticks (the "snow") — the textures and flavors vary delightfully with each mouthful. *Almond Duck,* steamed, deep-fried, and coated with sweet-sour sauce, is moist and rich.

Noodle dishes are good here. Try *Mushroom Chicken Noodles,* deep-fried yee mein ("long life" noodles) in a light sauce with mushrooms and chicken, or *Shrimp Chow Fun,* flat rice noodles, Chinese broccoli, and shrimp stir-fried together — this is a dish that gives balance to a meal with spicy foods.

GRAND PALACE

950 Grant Avenue (between Jackson and Washington)
982-3705
Cuisine: Cantonese and dim sum (lunch only)
Price range: Moderate
Hours: 9 A.M. – 10 P.M. daily
Credit cards: MasterCard, Visa
Full bar from 5 P.M.

The Grand Palace is saved from austerity by attractive wood paneling and brown, silver, and orange wallpaper, and the menu reflects some differences from the usual Chinese restaurant fare.

There is a good variety of seafood here, especially *Shrimp with Szechuan Sauce* and *Stir-fry Scallops;* the former is sautéed with mixed vegetables in a hot, spicy sauce, and the latter is quickly cooked with vegetables, retaining the sweet flavor of the scallops.

There is also an excellent version of *Lemon Chicken:* boneless pieces dipped in batter and deep-fried, and served with a tangy lemon sauce that includes thin slices of the fruit.

A beef specialty is *Wu-Nam Beef:* thin slices sautéed in hot, peppery bean sauce with julienned carrots, yellow onions, bamboo shoots, and black mushrooms.

GREAT WALL RESTAURANT

815 Washington Street (between Grant and Waverly)
397-5826
Cuisine: Cantonese
Price range: Moderate
Hours: 11–10, closed Tuesday
No credit cards
Beer only

From the street level, this appears to be a small, plain, and thoroughly unassuming place, but there is a cheery, slightly garish dining room upstairs, graced (if that is the right word) by elaborately gilded beams, heavy on dragons and bright colors.

The menu is fairly extensive. One of the outstanding specialties is *Hong Toe Yee Ton,* well-stuffed deep-fried won ton served in a flavorful soup of chicken stock with egg, cilantro, green onion, mushrooms, and something zesty.

Village Style Sautéed Clams come in the shell, with a tasty but subtle sauce — if you want spiciness, ask that some chili peppers be added. *Fried Squid,* coated with batter and lightly deep-fried, is also good as an appetizer.

Crispy Chicken is listed only on the Chinese menu. It is half a plump chicken coated in a honey-based glaze and then deep-fried; the tender, juicy meat with its dark-brown crisp skin is then chopped into serving pieces. The Chinese tend to undercook chicken and prefer it with the juices running pink, so you may want to order it well-done. It is served with salt flavored with five spice powder.

Abalone Slice Sautéed in Oyster Sauce is canned abalone, fairly tender and quite tasty. *Beef with Snow Peas* is marinated in a light brown sauce, then sautéed; it's seasonal. *Beef with Tender Greens* is a good alternative.

As we said, the menu is quite extensive; perhaps we should say both menus. The waiters are helpful, and this would be one place to take a chance and ask them to add something of their choice from the Chinese menu to your meal.

IMPERIAL PALACE

919 Grant Avenue (between Washington and Jackson)
982-4440
Cuisine: Cantonese
Price range: Expensive
Hours: Sun—Thurs 11:30 A.M.—1 A.M.,
       Fri—Sat 11:30 A.M.—2 A.M.
All major credit cards
Full bar

The Imperial Palace is Chinatown's luxury restaurant, first-class all the way: fine pink napery, exquisite china and decor, subdued lighting, tuxedoed waiters, bound wine lists, rolling carts for tableside service, not a chopstick in sight, and the sweet smell of success everywhere.

The food is quite well prepared, as it should be at these prices, and the wine list is the best in Chinatown (and better than many places outside it).

A glaring incongruity here, however, is that so much of the thrust of the place is Western that it's out of kilter, like a beautiful woman with one brown and one blue eye. The effect is unsettling — and the food generally consists of terrific renditions of standard Cantonese fare though for what you're paying, something more exalted would be in order.

For a special occasion, especially if you like good wine, we recommend three lobster dishes, which are actually the best values on the menu: *Lobster Kwangtung, Lobster in Black Bean Sauce,* and *Lobster Imperial.*

JACKSON CAFE

640 Jackson Street (between Kearny and Grant)
986-9717, 982-2409
Cuisine: Cantonese and American
Price range: Inexpensive
Hours: 11–10 daily
No credit cards
Beer and sometimes wine

The Jackson, as it is affectionately known, looks like a coffee shop anywhere in the Midwest, all Formica and Naugahyde and brightly lighted, with a long counter down one wall and booths down the other, and a few tables in the back. Years ago, when it was open till late at night, you could often see Chinese and hippies and guys in tuxedos side by side at the counter over a midnight snack. Today, the cross-section is a little narrower.

One thing that has never changed is that they serve the best clams in Chinatown, either in garlic sauce or black bean sauce and both outstanding; they are called "steamed," but are actually sautéed in the sauce and served in large steel bowls.

Steamed Rock Cod is almost always available, though not listed on the menu. It's a whole fish, quite fresh, steamed with slivers of green onion and ginger, then finished with a shower of hot oil and soy sauce and served up in a large bowl. Only another fish could love the way it looks, but it is tender, moist, and delicious. Another version is sliced, deep-fried, and served with sweet and sour sauce, but it's much like a gilded lily.

Pan-fried Sand Dabs are also served whole and golden brown, in a light Chinese gravy; it's worth fiddling with the bones to enjoy the flavor. In season, *Asparagus Beef* is sensational: the asparagus is barely cooked and generously portioned.

There are a lot of other interesting-looking dishes served here. The American menu changes constantly and some folks swear by it, but since the clams are a must and the fish is so good, we have to admit that our noble intentions always go awry and we stay happily in our rut.

JUNMAE GUEY

1222 Stockton Street (between Broadway and Pacific)
433-3981
Cuisine: Cantonese
Price range: Inexpensive
Hours: 8–6, closed Wednesday
No credit cards

Junmae Guey does a heavy business in take-out foods; from the street, it looks as if that is all they do, but there are also a dozen small tables in the back. It's very popular, so the relatively simple food is always fresh; and it's cheap, so it's usually crowded, if not chaotic — assertiveness training will be helpful here.

Won Ton in Supreme Soup is especially good, with a large amount of shrimp in the filling; the menu doesn't say so, but you can order barbecued pork strips or beef slices at a small extra charge as a garnish. *Won Ton and Noodle Soup* is a variation, quite filling.

Shredded Pork with Noodles and Hot Pepper Sauce is listed under "Noodles in Soup," but doesn't contain much liquid; it's hot and spicy and good. *Rice Noodles with Beef and Soy Sauce* is also quite hot, and very good.

There are fifteen different rice plates offered. We recommend *Black Bean Sauce Spareribs, Beef and Tender Greens, Chicken with Tender Greens, Roast Duck, Barbecued Pork,* and *Scrambled Eggs and Beef* (the eggs are very smooth, lightly cooked eggs, somewhat runny and very tasty).

There is also a selection of congees, the rice gruel cooked in chicken broth, with various additions cooked into it at the last minute, quite hearty and an incredible bargain; not in the least fancy, of course, but great on a cold day. Try *Chicken Congee, Beef Congee, Sliced Fresh Fish and Meatball Congee,* or for the truly adventuresome, *Variety Meat Congee* (liver, tripe, pork meatballs, and chicken).

KAM LOK

834 Washington Street (between Grant and Stockton)
421-8102
Cuisine: Cantonese
Price range: Inexpensive to moderate
Hours: 11—midnight daily
No credit cards
Beer and wine

Kam Lok is downstairs, plain but attractive, and usually
bustling. It offers, basically, good simple food and good value.
Quite a few noodle dishes and rice plates are featured.

A meal here starts with a small bowl of soup plunked down in
front of you whether you order it or not—thin chicken stock, some
bits of meat, some seaweed perhaps; a plastic glass of tea will also
be served you. There is no charge for either.

Among the rice plates, *Curry Sam See* is a good choice. The
Chinese have traded with India for thousands of years and have
adopted curry, but with a slightly less heavy hand than their
neighbors. This dish consists of strips of chicken, mushrooms,
bamboo shoots, celery, and yellow onion on a mountain of white
rice. It can also be ordered as a side dish.

There are a number of good dishes on the Chinese menu. *Boiled
Shrimp* come in the shell, with a soy and jalapeño pepper sauce for
dipping; *Deep-fried Stuffed Bean Cake* is fresh tofu stuffed with fish
paste, deep-fried, and served in a light gravy; *Stir-fried Beef Strips*
are marinated in a good, spicy sauce and go well with plain
steamed rice; *King Tu Spareribs* are dipped in a light batter, deep-
fried till crisp, and served in a sweet-sour sauce containing
Chinese pickled vegetables.

The cryptic menus don't give much hint of this, but Kam Lok
is also a terrific place for seafood — notice the tanks full of fish
near the kitchen. Waiters here are young and helpful, and will be
happy to recommend whatever is best that day.

LICHEE GARDEN

1416 Powell Street (between Broadway and Vallejo)
397-2290
Cuisine: Cantonese and Mandarin
Price range: Moderate
Hours: 11:30–9:30 daily
Credit cards: MasterCard, Visa
Beer and wine

The Lichee Garden is fairly new and already popular, deservedly
so. The extensive menu has interesting specialties, the portions
are generous, and the prices are quite reasonable.

It's an uncommonly attractive place, with partitions
surmounted by potted plants, attractive hanging lamps, and full
carpeting that helps to keep the noise level down.

Two soups are outstanding. *Shredded Scallop Soup* contains
shredded dried scallops, shredded chicken, bamboo shoots,
mushrooms, and egg drop in a slightly thickened chicken stock.
West Lake Beef Soup is not listed in the menu; it contains minced
beef, bamboo shoots, water chestnuts, cilantro, and beaten egg in
a thickened chicken stock base. Both of these are hearty.

Lichee Garden Special Spareribs (also known as *Chun-Kang
Spareribs*) are actually pork chops sliced very thin, dipped in a very
light batter, deep-fried, and finished in a unique sauce that is
slightly sweet and totally delicious. The bite-sized pieces are best
eaten with the fingers.

Beef with Walnuts is very much a winner. Julienned onions are
also an ingredient, and the whole is united by a spicy sauce that
doesn't get in the way of the delightfully odd marriage of flavors.
Other good dishes that would balance a meal are *Mongolian Beef or
Lamb,* with green and yellow onion and a sweet-h
sauce, and *Kung Pao Prawns or Chicken,* both excel
this dish.

There is also a good selection of clay-pot dishes
menu; we recommend *Ambassador Li-Hung Chong*
and *Spring Ginger and Pineapple and Honey with Ch*
waiters here are very helpful, so perhaps the best
their advice about one of these to fill out a meal.

LOTUS GARDEN

532 Grant Avenue (between Pine and California)
397-0130
Cuisine: Vegetarian
Price range: Moderate
Hours: 11–10 daily
All major credit cards
Full bar

The highly creative cooking here is likely to change your perceptions of vegetarian food forever; the vegetables are crisp and *al dente,* the sauces authoritatively flavorful, and the combinations imaginative.

Lotus Garden is on the second floor, away from the bustle of the street outside, with an elegantly understated decor: cool green walls, white napery, and sparkling chandeliers. Service is attentive and the pace is unhurried.

The menu is long and varied. There is a good selection of soups and noodle dishes, but, as the portions are generous, it's best to go easy on them as appetizers—each should be counted as one dish toward the total for the number of diners.

Sweet and Sour Walnuts doesn't appear on the menu, but is frequently available on request; walnuts are dipped in batter and deep-fried, then served topped with a light sweet-sour sauce—don't miss it. *Gluten Puff Balls* appear in various vegetable combinations and sauces, and are worth a try. The gluten is overworked wheat flour that forms a slightly heavy (glutinous) ball resembling an oyster in shape and consistency, and it absorbs the flavor of whatever sauce it's served in; one good version is with green pepper and spicy black bean sauce.

Another nice dish is *Fried Taro,* in which taro root is steamed and mashed, pressed into an exquisitely decorated fish shape, then deep-fried till golden; its sweet flavor complements many of the other dishes' sauces. *Black Mushrooms with Broccoli* is another good combination, served with oyster sauce. There are also several combinations of vegetables and rice noodles that are outstanding.

There are quite a few varieties of tea available to round out a most interesting menu.

On the third floor is a beautiful Taoist temple, elaborately and quite colorfully decorated, well worth a quiet visit. It, like the restaurant below, is under the supervision of the Ching Chung Taoist Association of America, and it is open seven days a week, from 11:00 A.M. to 8:00 P.M. Mr. Lee, the pastor, speaks good English and is most happy to show visitors around and answer questions.

LOUIE'S

1014 Grant Avenue (between Jackson and Pacific)
982-5762
Cuisine: Cantonese and dim sum
Price range: Moderate
Hours: 9:30 A.M.–midnight daily
(dim sum 9:30 A.M.–2:30 P.M. daily)
No credit cards
Full bar

You climb a flight of narrow stairs that does nothing to prepare you for the enormous dining rooms on the second and third floors, the former for dinners and the latter for lunches, both as barren as an army barracks. Louie's has been around quite awhile, and has clearly seen better days, but the kitchen still rises to the occasion.

Steamed Fish is moist and flavorful in a plain version topped with green onion, ginger, and soy sauce; a version with black bean sauce is also a notch above the usual.

Crispy Chicken, deep-fried but tender, is listed only on the Chinese menu, as are *Stir-fried Chicken in Hot Bean Sauce* and *Stir-fried Scallops.* Both come with vegetables; the former is quite hot, while the latter is tender and sweet.

This is one place where waiters are happy to take a customized order for fried noodles and various meats and vegetables — in fact, they may suggest some delightful combinations if you encourage them.

MANDARIN DELIGHT

941 Kearny Street (at Columbus)
362-8299
Cuisine: Mandarin and Szechuan
Price range: Moderate
Hours: 11:30—9:30, closed Thursday
All major credit cards
Beer and wine

From the outside, Mandarin Delight looks like just another store-front, but inside is a large room with a high ceiling and wood paneling along one wall; the tables aren't crammed together, either, so it looks and feels spacious.

It has quite an extensive menu for a place that isn't that large or possessed of many pretensions. There is a list of house specialties up front on the menu, and they are good bets. *Green Onion Pancakes* are a fine start.

Ants on a Tree is an offbeat version of a Szechuan classic; here it is ground beef cooked in a thick hot sauce with fine-chopped red peppers, tossed together with deep-fried rice sticks that have been broken up, and served accompanied with ice-cold lettuce leaves — two tablespoons or so are spooned into the leaves, which are then rolled up and eaten.

Jade Chicken is wonderful, crispy chicken in a ginger-garlic sauce with green onion and chopped Chinese greens, very spicy without being overwhelmingly hot. *Phoenix Chicken in a Basket* (or a shrimp version) is also a little offbeat. The basket is shredded taro root, and the filling is marinated in a kung pao sauce that is hot without being fiery. It's a very successful dish. In fact, whoever makes the sauces here deserves an award.

Another odd but interesting dish is on the vegetable menu, called *Green Sheets*. It isn't green, and the sheets are rice flour, but it's a good menu-balancer. It is served cold, the sheets inter-spersed with shredded chicken and julienned cucumber, and the whole tossed together in a ground-peanut sauce — refreshing and definitely unique.

The service is also friendly. All in all, there is enough about the menu and cooking here to make it worth repeat visits.

OCEAN GARDEN

735 Jackson Street (between Grant and Stockton)
421-9129
Cuisine: Cantonese
Price range: Moderate
Hours: 11:30 A.M. – 1 A.M. daily
No credit cards

Ocean Garden is relatively new, plain, small, and cramped; the service is offhand. The food, however, is pretty good.

Both *West Lake Beef Soup* and *Diced Chicken with Corn Soup* are hearty and flavorful and worth trying. *Chicken with Black Bean* is half a seasoned chicken sautéed in a black bean sauce, quite tender and juicy.

From the Chinese menu, *Filet of Sole* is excellent: chunks of sole stir-fried with a light sauce. Many of the specials on the Chinese menu are fish, and it's worth the bother of negotiating with the waiter for at least one recommendation.

Also from the Chinese menu is a good selection of clay-pot dishes. We recommend *Roast Pork and Rock Cod with Minced Garlic* (much better than it sounds), and *Bean Cake with Assorted Meats,* containing deep-fried bean cake, gizzards, squid, shrimp, chicken, barbecued pork, mushrooms, and water chestnuts in a good sauce.

OCEAN SKY

641 Jackson Street (between Grant and Kearny)
433-6802, 433-6803
Cuisine: Cantonese, dim sum (lunch only), vegetarian
Price range: Moderate
Hours: Mon–Fri 8:30 A.M.–3 A.M., Sat–Sun 7 A.M.–3 A.M.
    (dim sum 8:30 A.M.–3 P.M. daily)
No credit cards
Beer and wine

Ocean Sky looks like a plain and modest restaurant from the front door, but two back rooms usually guarantee you a seat, and the talent in the kitchen is all the embellishment it needs.

The family that operates Ocean Sky has been involved with restaurants in Chinatown for some time, but is now clearly staking out some culinary turf of its own here. Among the usual Cantonese staples can be found some interesting variations; the seafood list is especially good, and a *Special Seafood Dinner* is a fine introduction to its possibilities, featuring a soup and five seafood dishes for approximately thirty dollars—it feeds five people well.

The restaurant also features fifteen vegetarian dishes; we especially recommend *Snow Peas and Water Chestnuts, Bean Cake with Three Mushrooms,* and *Cashew Nuts and Three Sliced Vegetables.*

Two dishes usually featured on the Chinese menu are well worth asking about. *King Tu Pork* is pieces of meat about the size of your little finger, some with bones in, dipped in a light batter, deep-fried, and then tossed in a sweet, spicy sauce. *Taro Basket with Beef Strips* is a spectacular presentation of shredded taro root shaped like a basket, deep-fried, then filled with stir-fried beef strips and mixed vegetables.

For the adventuresome, there is *Oyster with Ginger and Green Onion:* fresh oysters gently stir-fried, still tender, enhanced by the onion-ginger flavor; if you have even the slightest affection for oysters it is worth a try.

THE POT STICKER

150 Waverly Place (between Washington and Clay)
397-9985
Cuisine: Mandarin
Price range: Moderate
Hours: 11:30–10 daily
Credit cards: MasterCard, Visa
Beer and wine

It is a small place and always looks impossibly crowded, but there is also a dining room downstairs. Of course, you should have *Pot Stickers* for a start. This is one of the few places that serves *Chinese Doughnuts* (which look like enormous crullers, and in a way are—just fried dough, delicious and oily); they are not on the menu, so you have to ask. *Hot and Sour Soup* is good here, in a thickened version that's nice and hearty.

Princess Chicken* is diced, mixed with plenty of peanuts and sautéed in a hot bean sauce; *Mongolian Beef* is thin slices sautéed with carrots, celery, and green onions in hoisin sauce—sweet and spicy at once; *Orange Spareribs* are coated in a thick, rich honey-orange sauce, good as a component in a multicourse meal. *Tan Tan Noodles* are topped with ground pork, peas, and green onions in a spicy sauce; mix well before tucking in.

SHEW WO CAFE

667 Jackson Street (between Grant and Kearny)
956-8019
Cuisine: American
Price range: Inexpensive
Hours: 7:30 A.M.–9 P.M., closed Monday
No credit cards

Among the Chinese, it is fairly fashionable to go out for American food once in awhile, and this is the kind of cuisine served at Shew Wo: the menu could be lifted from any coffee shop in the Midwest. Even the ever-changing daily specials are basic American food, and so is most of what is listed on the Chinese-language menu.

One thing that is different about this place, however, is that the food is better for the price than you are liable to find in most similar places anywhere else in town, especially at breakfast. Save room for the warm apple pie featured here. The only flaw is the coffee; the tea, of course, is first-rate.

SUN HUNG HEUNG

744 Washington Street (between Kearny and Grant)
982-2319
Cuisine: Cantonese
Price range: Moderate
Hours: 11:30 A.M.—midnight, closed Tuesday
Credit cards: MasterCard, Visa
Full bar

It is unassuming and small downstairs, but there is a large upstairs dining room, partitioned areas, that is quite pleasant. Either way, the service is friendly and solicitous, and the food is good.

To begin with, the *Shark's Fin Soup* here is the best in town; it is not listed on the menu, but is available at about six dollars a serving (the price varies) and worth it.

Cantonese Chicken Salad is well executed. Shredded cold fried chicken (crispy skin included) is served with shredded iceberg lettuce, celery, green onion, and snow peas in season, in a house dressing topped with toasted sesame seeds, deep-fried peanuts, and crisp deep-fried rice sticks, garnished with cilantro.

Fried Stuffed Chicken Wings are not what you might expect. The chicken wings are boned down to the tips, and a forcemeat stuffing of ground chicken meat, pork, mushrooms, and water chestnuts is packed back into the skin; the wings are then deep-fried until golden brown, sliced, and served in a shallow pool of brown gravy (which is, it should be noted, dull and unnecessary — don't muddle the wings around in it, just lift them away). This dish is a rarity and, as the wings are three or four times their original size and quite rich, not to be taken lightly.

Other notable dishes are *Clams in Black Bean Sauce* or *Clams in Garlic Sauce, Steak Cubes with Chinese Broccoli,* and *Steamed Whole Fish.*

Portions here are particularly generous, so it's a good value; if you order a noodle dish, order the "small" portion — you'll get what passes for the normal portion most other places.

SUN WAH KUE

848 Washington Street (between Grant and Stockton)
982-3519
Cuisine: American
Price range: Inexpensive
Hours: 7 A.M.—8 P.M., closed Tuesday
No credit cards

Sun Wah Kue has been in business for over fifty years, and in many ways looks it. It's as plain and unpretentious as a restaurant can be, even in Chinatown, and its smallish size is reduced by a row of enclosed booths along one wall.

The food is straight-ahead American diner fare — steaks, chops, chicken, mashed potatoes, a vegetable of the day, fresh rolls and butter, coffee and pie — all rather plain, all included in the four- or five-dollar price listed for each entrée, all hearty portions; sometimes rice is the starch, and tea is available, but they don't seem appropriate in this palace of incongruity. Corned beef and cabbage is also available — why not? A specialty of the house is slabs of prime rib, a great bargain, always sold out by 1 P.M.

The restaurant also includes an excellent bakery featuring a notable, old-fashioned apple pie, cheaper than anything comparable in town.

Given the fact that everything is made fresh every day from scratch, this may be one of the best bargains in town; be forewarned that the locals are quite aware of that.

TONG KEE No. 1

854 Washington Street (between Grant and Stockton)
982-0936
Hours: 10:30 A.M.—1 A.M. daily

TONG KEE No. 2

1365 Stockton Street (corner of Vallejo)
956-8336
Hours: 10:30—9 daily

TONG KEE No. 3

710 Kearny Street (near Washington)
982-5341, 982-5342
Hours: 10:30—9 daily
Cuisine: Cantonese
Price range: Inexpensive
No credit cards

Tong Kee began in Hong Kong as a classic unpretentious place
featuring noodles and won ton dishes, and has flourished here
with the same kind of menu and no-frills atmosphere. It's quick,
cheap, authentic, and good.

One and Three are relatively small and frequently crowded,
best for a quick snack or lunch if you arrive before noon. Two is
larger and more attractive since a recent remodeling and features a
more extensive menu; it also tends to be crowded.

There is a good selection of congees at all three, and we
recommend beef, chicken, prawn, abalone and chicken, and
abalone and prawn. A range of won ton soups is also available, all
with noodles added. *Shrimp Won Ton* is excellent. At a slight extra
cost, order a garnish of barbecued pork or roast duck.

Fried Clams are stir-fried in either black bean or garlic sauce,
and the portion is generous, making this a real bargain. *Ginger
Beef* is slices of meat sautéed with slivered ginger, quite spicy and
good. *Chicken with Black Mushrooms* is heavy on the mushrooms,
which are stewed in a rich chicken stock to which chicken is then
added; the gravy is wonderful with steamed rice.

There is also a large selection of clay-pot dishes, and we
recommend *Roast Duck with Prawns,* and *Prawns with Ginger and
Green Onion, Chicken,* or *Ox Tongue.* Each is made with different
vegetables and sauces, but all are worth trying.

TON KIANG

683 Broadway (between Stockton and Grant)
421-2015
Cuisine: Hakka
Price range: Moderate
Hours: 11 A.M.—midnight daily
Credit cards: MasterCard, Visa
Beer only

Hakka cuisine is rare in San Francisco, and this is a good example
of it. The Hakka people were driven from their homes in northern
China thousands of years ago. They migrated to an area near
Canton, but retained their language and customs; their cuisine
underwent some transformation, but is still distinctive.

For one thing, they are the only Chinese who cook with
appreciable amounts of wine. A good introduction is any of the
three wine-based soups, beef, chicken, or pork. The pink things
floating in them are grains of short-grain rice fermented with
wine yeast, and the predominant flavor is a pleasant, mildly
vinegarlike sourness.

Another specialty, listed as *Fish Ball,* consists of rather bland
balls of fish paste pan-fried, then sliced and sautéed with Chinese
greens—a triumph of flavor over language.

The most popular dish here, deservedly so, is *Salt-baked
Chicken.* The cooking process is almost as laborious in the
description as in the making; suffice it to say that you get half a
golden chicken (cut up) that is as tender and juicy as is humanly
possible, only slightly salty, and quite delicious. There is also a
good version of *Crispy Fried Chicken.*

A small dish of piquant orange-colored sauce is served with the
chicken, meant for dipping. How hot is it? A few ounces could
have held off the Mongol hordes indefinitely.

The next most popular dish is *Braised Rock Cod,* especially
nicely done here. *Crystal Prawns,* not found on very many menus,
are shelled and served in a light sauce with snow peas and carrot
slices.

Two good menu-balancers here would be *Fried Bean Curd with
Stuffed Meat,* ground pork tucked into triangles of bean curd,
deep-fried, and served with brown gravy; and *Beef in Szechuan
Sauce,* strips of beef sautéed with vegetables in a hot bean sauce.

YA SU YUAN

638 Pacific Avenue (between Grant and Kearny)
986-7386
Cuisine: Mandarin and Szechuan
Price range: Moderate
Hours: 11:30 – 10 daily
Credit card: MasterCard
Beer and wine

Ya Su Yuan is two long rooms, side by side, with partitions between; one room features a long photomural of autumn woods, the other has white walls adorned with attractive paintings — both are visual pleasures, carpeted and comfortable.

The menu seems unimaginative, but the cooking is not — many of the apparently familiar dishes are executed in delightfully offbeat ways. Try *Hot Spiced String Beans* and see what we mean: the beans are stir-fried in hot sauce with red pepper, but pieces of crumbled bacon are mixed in to add an interesting fillip.

Pot Stickers and *Mu Shi Pork* are both outstanding, perfect versions of what too often is a cliché elsewhere. *Szechuan Prawns* is another dish that is a cut above the ordinary.

All the Szechuan dishes are spiced perfectly, treading the line between merely spicy and taking the top of your head off.

Another interesting feature of the menu is three desserts rarely seen elsewhere, denoted "glaced." They are bananas, apples, and lichees that are dipped in melted sugar, then plunged into cold water so that the sugar forms a light glaze. They embody the Chinese ideal of beauty in simplicity.

Dim Sum

Yum cha is the Chinese tea lunch featuring dim sum, which means "touching the heart." San Francisco's dim sum restaurants are rated the best in the world.

There are several dozen delicacies in the dim sum repertoire, usually served three to a plate, each one a hearty mouthful. Thus eight or nine dishes shared among at least three people makes a good light lunch. There is a variety of dumplings, rolls, buns, small casseroles, meatballs, unidentified frying objects, and sweets; we have listed and described some of the most common below.

Most dim sum restaurants serve from about nine in the morning until three in the afternoon, but it's best to get to them before noon. A cook's shift starts before dawn and ends a little before noon, so when the restaurant runs out of some kinds of food, no more is made (new cooks who come on duty at noon generally make noodle dishes and other light foods and get ready for dinner). Also, these places usually fill up by noon and there can be a long wait unless you are willing to share a larger table.

In the evening, you usually get no choice of tea in Chinese restaurants, but with dim sum there is generally a good variety available. Po Nay is a mild black tea that is a particular favorite; Lok On and Lichee are two others. Loon Jaing, or Dragon's Well, is the green tea you should ask for if you like a milder tea — they are all brewed a bit stronger for tea lunch. Incidentally, when your teapot is empty, simply turn the lid upside down, which is the universal sign that you want a refill; the usual charge for any of these teas is 50¢ per person, with no charge for a refill.

Getting into the spirit of a dim sum lunch can take a little doing. There is usually a fair amount of noise and confusion (or at least apparent confusion), there is no menu, and gentility will not get you very far. Waitresses wheel around carts of hot food, sometimes singing out the foods they offer, sometimes not, and if they do, it's in Chinese. They will stop by your table, lift the lids of the various canisters and bamboo steamers, show you unrecognizable foods, and urge you to try them; their English is frequently not very good, but they want you to enjoy and will often cajole you into trying something.

Dim sum is worth the effort, however. There are a lot of pleasant surprises, and, as you're having tidbits, you can't go very far wrong. It's easy, in fact, to fall into a feeding frenzy and ask for at least one plate of everything that goes by. Pacing yourself and being choosy is important; the waitresses are not offended if you turn down their offerings, and in the normal roundelay of things, everything comes up again at least once; the thing is to pick and choose and stay loose.

If you want a noodle dish or some other regular food to supplement the dim sum, just ask for a menu and order it.

When you are finished, a waiter or waitress will count up the dishes on your table and calculate your check. Each dish (usually containing three tidbits) costs about $1.20.

Dim sum lunches also are a nice solution to the problem of eating alone. Most restaurants set aside a table or two for singles or couples willing to share with other people, so you are not left staring into space or reading a book while you wait to be served.

One other tip: Try to sit as near the kitchen as possible, if you have a choice — in some of the larger restaurants, that will guarantee hot food at its best (during peak times, you may not have a choice about seating, of course, in which case you should take from fuller carts, rather than those with only a few dishes, whose waitresses may have been wandering for too long).

DIM SUM SPECIALTIES

Baked Barbecued Pork Buns

Browned yeast rolls, filled with barbecued pork and yellow onion.

Beef Dumplings

Seasoned minced beef wrapped in round dumpling skins; steamed.

Beef Meatballs

Seasoned minced beef steamed over watercress.

Black Bean Spareribs

Bite-sized pork spareribs marinated in Chinese seasonings and steamed with salted black beans.

Chinese Doughnuts

Glutinous rice-flour dough filled with sweet bean paste, sprinkled with sesame seeds, and fried.

Custard Cups

Pastry tarts with a light lemon custard filling. (We hope you will try one of these. They are especially good.)

Egg Rolls

Slivered barbecued pork, bamboo shoots, green onions, bean sprouts, and button mushrooms wrapped in egg roll skins and deep-fried.

Half-Moon Dumplings

Wheat-starch dough filled with minced pork, shrimp, carrots, and peas; steamed.

Pork Dumplings

Minced pork and shrimp wrapped in round dumpling skins; steamed.

Pork Triangles

A filling of minced pork, mushrooms, shrimp, and bamboo shoots wrapped in a rice-flour dough and deep-fried.

Rice Casserole with Chicken

Pieces of seasoned chicken, mushrooms, and Chinese sausage, cooked in a rice casserole.

Rice Casserole with Spareribs

Seasoned spareribs with salted black beans cooked in a rice casserole.

Shrimp Dumplings

Wheat-starch dough filled with minced shrimp and bamboo shoots; steamed.

Steamed Barbecued Pork Buns

White steamed buns filled with seasoned barbecued pork.

Stuffed Bean Cake

Fresh bean cake stuffed with shrimp mixture, pan-fried, and served with brown gravy.

Stuffed Bell Peppers

Pieces of bell pepper filled with minced shrimp, fried, and topped with brown gravy.

Stuffed Rice-Flour Rolls

Sheets of rice noodle stuffed with minced beef, barbecued pork, or shrimp, rolled like a jelly roll and steamed.

Taro Root Triangles

A minced pork, mushroom, and shrimp filling wrapped in mashed cooked taro, dipped in batter, and deep-fried.

Dim Sum Restaurants

ASIA GARDEN
772 Pacific Avenue (between Grant and Stockton)
398-5112
Hours: 9—3 daily

CANTON TEA HOUSE
1108 Stockton Street (between Pacific and Jackson)
982-1030
Hours: 7—3 daily

CELADON
881 Clay Street (between Grant and Stockton)
982-1168
Hours: 9—3 daily

GOLDEN DRAGON RESTAURANT
822 Washington Street (between Grant and Stockton)
398-3920
Hours: 9—3 daily

GOLDEN PAVILION
800 Sacramento Street (at Grant)
392-2334
Hours: 11—2:30 daily

GRAND PALACE
950 Grant Avenue (between Jackson and Washington)
982-3705
Hours: 9—2:30 daily

HANG AH
1 Pagoda Place (near Stockton)
982-5686
Hours: 10—3 daily

HONG KONG TEA HOUSE

835 Pacific Avenue (between Stockton and Powell)
391-6365
Hours: 9—3 daily

LOUIE'S

1014 Grant Avenue (between Jackson and Pacific)
982-5762
Hours: 9:30—2:30 daily

OCEAN SKY

641 Jackson Street (between Grant and Kearny)
433-6802
Hours: 8:30—3 daily

RUBY PALACE

631 Kearny Street (near Washington)
433-3196
Hours: Mon—Fri 11:30—2:30, Sat—Sun 11—2:30

TUNG FONG

808 Pacific Avenue (between Stockton and Powell)
362-7115
Hours: 9—3, closed Wednesday

YANK SING RESTAURANT

671 Broadway (between Columbus and Stockton)
781-1111
Hours: 10—3 daily

The Food Shops
of Chinatown

To an outsider, the teeming streets and markets of Chinatown can be intimidating, but it's worth penetrating the bustle and mystery because the Chinese are extremely demanding about the quality of their food and you will benefit from their standards. Also, prices tend to be lower than elsewhere in town. Most markets are open on Sundays, another benefit.

TAKE-OUTS

The windows of every market in Chinatown are decked with trays of a wide and exotic variety of prepared foods. Both culturally and of necessity (many apartment houses still have tiny communal kitchens, if they have kitchens at all), cooked food "to go" is a staple here.

Roast duck and chicken, barbecued pork and spareribs, and fried chicken are ubiquitous; some places also feature pei pa duck, roast squab, and roast pig. The other prepared dishes, especially stews, may change with the seasons and availability of various foods. Many of the stews make for a good quick lunch, especially with steamed rice. (There is one that looks as if it is composed mostly of pigs' tails. It is.)

The Chinese love to tell the story of how roast pig began: It seems that one day a peasant's hut burned down with his pig inside. As the farmer poked around the ashes, he burned his fingers on the pig's corpse, plunged them into his mouth, and discovered how delicious the taste was. After that, every time he wanted this delicacy, he burned down his hut with a pig inside.

Today, it's easier. Several Chinatown markets sell whole roast pigs, young ones that average about fifty pounds (tender, and without an abundance of fat). Whole pigs may be ordered in advance, and you can specify the approximate weight and whether you'd like it cut up in serving pieces, which are then rearranged on a wooden serving tray. These shops also usually have a pig cut up, from which the casual shopper can buy pieces, including the crisp skin.

You should not expect to pay by check or credit card in these shops. They accept cash only.

Here are some of the specialties you might wish to search out:

Roast Duck: Duck marinated in Chinese seasonings with parsley, then roasted till brown. It is *not* Peking Duck, which is found only in restaurants. You may purchase a whole duck (price: about $8) or a half. Have the clerk cut it into manageable pieces.

To serve, bring the roasting juices, sold with the duck, to a boil and pour over the cold duck. It will keep, refrigerated, for about three days.

Pei Pa Duck: This duck is drier and crisper, more like Peking Duck, steeped in a sweeter marinade before roasting. It is not available in all shops, so we have indicated those that carry it. The bird has been cut open and flattened, and you must buy it whole (price: about $8). To serve, roast in a 325-degree oven for thirty minutes, then cut into serving pieces. It is sold without roasting juices, but plum sauce is an excellent accompaniment. It will keep about three days in the refrigerator.

Roast Chicken: Chicken marinated in Chinese seasonings with parsley, then roasted; quite delicious. You may purchase a whole chicken (price: about $6), a half, or a quarter. To serve, chop into serving pieces (or have the clerk do it). Heat the roasting juices, sold with the chicken, and pour over the cold chicken. Will keep about three days if refrigerated.

Soy Sauce Chicken: This is simmered in soy sauce with sugar and spices. It is displayed on a tray. A whole chicken costs about $6, but you may buy as little as a quarter. Have the clerk cut it into serving pieces. The cooking juices are especially tasty; heat and pour over the cold chicken. This dish goes especially well with steamed rice. It will keep about three days in the refrigerator.

Boiled Chicken: This is simmered in stock, without spices, and is milder in flavor than other chicken dishes. It is a very popular dish for Chinese New Year. A whole chicken is about $6, but you may purchase as little as a quarter. It comes without any juices, and is good cold, with oyster sauce. It will keep about three days, refrigerated.

Barbecued Pork: Lean pork marinated in special, slightly sweet seasonings, then barbecued. It sells for about $4 per pound. You can ask the clerk to cut off a piece for you, which will sometimes weigh less than half a pound. It may be eaten "as is" (sliced, it makes a delightful hors d'oeuvre), or julienned and combined with vegetables, or added to noodle soup, fried rice, or chow mein. It may also be reheated in a 325-degree oven for ten minutes. It will keep a week in the refrigerator, or may be frozen for up to three months.

Barbecued Spareribs: Prepared in a similar manner to barbecued pork, and has the same keeping time. Reheat in a 325-degree oven for about ten minutes. (Price: about $3.50 per pound.)

Roast Pig: This delicacy is not available in every shop, so we have tried to indicate where it is sold. It is sold by weight, for approximately $4 per pound, but you may buy less than a pound. You may not be able to choose the part you prefer; look over the part that has been cut into, to judge how fat or lean it is. If it's not a good buy right there, try elsewhere or come back later. This treat is great for munching "as is," or as an accompaniment to rice. It will keep in the refrigerator for one week, or may be frozen for up to three months.

Cashew Nut Chicken: Contains chicken pieces, bamboo shoots, water chestnuts, celery, yellow onion, button mushrooms, sometimes snow peas, and deep-fried cashew nuts. Reheat before serving. This dish should be eaten the same day it is purchased, since the nuts become soggy if it's stored. (Price: about $3 per pound.)

Deep-fried Chicken: Usually drumsticks and wings, well-seasoned, dipped in a very light batter, then deep-fried. Colonel Sanders never had it so good. (Price: about $2 per pound.)

Mushrooms in Oyster Sauce: The mushrooms are simmered in stock, then oyster sauce is added. Since Chinese mushrooms are so expensive, the dish usually also contains button mushrooms, and sometimes green vegetables. To serve, reheat in a saucepan. Will keep in the refrigerator for about three days. (Price: about $3.50 per pound.)

Stuffed Bean Cake: This is fresh bean cake stuffed with fish paste and deep-fried. It comes with a brown gravy and looks like a very odd popover. To serve, reheat in a saucepan or microwave oven. It will keep in the refrigerator about two days. (Price: about $1.75 per pound.)

Jai (Monk's Stew): A vegetarian dish, traditional at Chinese New Year, but available every day. It contains mostly dried vegetables such as dried mushrooms, bamboo shoots, bean curd, lily flowers, fungus, bean threads, and fresh Napa cabbage. It is cooked with spices and red bean-curd paste. It may be reheated in a saucepan or in a microwave oven. It will keep in the refrigerator for about a week. (Price: about $2 per pound.)

Squid with Broccoli: Pieces of dried squid stir-fried (after sufficient soaking) with broccoli and Chinese seasonings. To reheat, stir-fry briefly. It will keep about three days in the refrigerator. (Price: about $2.80 per pound.)

Ox Tail Stew, Chinese style: Oxtails braised with Chinese seasonings and red bean curd. Sometimes combined with gingko nuts, dried bean curd, or dried mushrooms. Reheat in a saucepan or in a microwave oven. (Price: about $2.50 per pound.)

CANTON MARKET

1135 Stockton Street (between Pacific and Jackson)
982-8600
Hours: 9:30–5:30 daily
The usual take-out dishes, and pei pa duck.

DUPONT MARKET

1100 Grant Avenue (at Pacific)
986-3723
Hours: 9:30–5:30 daily
Usual dishes.

GOLDEN DAISY COMPANY

1041 Stockton Street (between Jackson and Washington)
392-0111
Hours: 9:30–6:30 daily
Roast pig available here, plus usual dishes.

GOLDEN DRAGON RESTAURANT

833 Washington Street (between Grant and Stockton)
Note: There are two Golden Dragon Restaurants, but this is the
one that has take-out food.
398-3920, 398-4550
Hours: 10:30–6 daily
Usual take-out dishes and roast pig.

HONG SANG MARKET

1136 Grant Avenue (between Broadway and Pacific)
982-4145
Hours: 9:30–5:30 daily
Usual take-out foods.

KUM YUEN RESTAURANT

1247 Stockton Street (near Broadway)
434-1128
Hours: 9:30–5:30 daily
Roast pig as well as the usual dishes.

ON SANG MARKET

1114 Grant Avenue (between Broadway and Pacific)
892-4694
Hours: 9:30—6 daily
Usual take-out dishes.

SHEW WO MARKET

1151 Stockton Street (near Pacific)
982-7235
Hours: 9:30—5:30 daily
Roast pig and the usual dishes.

SUN SANG MARKET

1205 Stockton Street (near Pacific)
989-3060
Hours: 9:30—5:30 daily
Roast pig and the usual dishes.

BAKERIES

The Chinese don't have any long-standing tradition of baking, but that hasn't stopped them from becoming very good at it. Chinatown bakeries turn out very good pies and cakes and other all-American delicacies at very good prices, and the Chinese specialties you will find are more than merely intriguing. Many bakers work a shift in some of the city's better bakeries and then put in another in Chinatown, or at least help out, so you are assured that some of the best talent in town is available. The pastries are lighter, because of a lower fat content, and the crusts on pies and tarts are as flaky as handmade should be.

One item found in Chinatown, the ham and egg bau, is a terrific meeting of East and West. The American ham and egg, baked into a Chinese roll, is a breakfast in itself.

Another delicacy you should try is the moon cake, served on the Festival of August Moon, August 15 of the lunar calendar (mid- or late September), and available for a month previously. This is a small cake, usually with a salted egg yolk in the center (although it is sometimes made without) symbolizing the August moon, a filling of nuts and fruits, and an embossed crust. It is traditional for younger generations to present moon cakes to older generations to denote respect. Also, large quantities of this same cake (but called "wedding cake" rather than moon cake) are presented by the family of the groom to the family of the bride about a month before the wedding.

Listed below are standard items usually found in bakeries. Each shop also has specialties that may be found only there, or perhaps only in one or two other establishments. None take checks or credit cards.

Pies: Apple, peach, custard, orange. (Price: about $2.)

Cakes: Strawberry, peach, banana, coconut, and the Chinatown specialty, peanut cake. (Most cakes are about $4.00.) Sponge cake is available plain or chocolate-flavored (about $2.00 each), or jelly-roll style with lemon filling (about $2.50). Pound cake comes plain, or with chopped walnuts mixed in (about $2.50).

Tarts: Coconut, sweetened bean, custard (about 50¢ each). The open lemon custard tart (often served with the Chinese tea lunch) contains no milk so is lower in cholesterol. Some resemble small buns, with Chinese ideographs stamped on them in red ink.

Cookies: Almond, sesame, and fortune cookies. Also cookies filled with winter melon, fruit and nut mixture, or sweet bean filling (about $3 per pound).

Moon Cakes: The most popular filling is made of lotus seeds. Other fillings available are sweet bean paste, coconut, or a mixture of nuts and preserved fruits. (Price: about $2.50 each.) Moon cakes are very rich and are served cut into wedges. One or two wedges per person is an adequate serving. Some shops have small versions for about 50¢.

Cocktail Buns: A sweet bun with cream filling, with shredded coconut sprinkled on top. (Price: about 50¢ each.) To serve cocktail buns the next day, reheat for half a minute in a microwave oven, or steam for eight minutes. (Do not reheat in a conventional oven!)

A.B.C. BAKERY

1068 Stockton Street (near Jackson)
981-0685
Hours: 7–6 daily
Specialties: Ham and egg bau, coconut tarts, and raisin buns (all about 50¢ each).

EASTERN BAKERY

720 Grant Avenue (corner of Commercial Street)
982-5157
Hours: 8–7 daily
Specialties: Coffee crunch cake (a very good buy at $5); moon cakes (about $2.50 each); coconut, lotus, and quite a few other tarts, all good.

MEE MEE BAKERY

1328 Stockton Street (between Vallejo and Broadway)
362-3204
Hours: 9–6, closed Sunday
Specialties: Fortune cookies, "adult" fortune cookies, almond cookies, sesame cookies, tea cookies.

NEW MAXIM'S BAKERY

1240 Stockton Street (near Broadway)
986-1660
Hours: 7—7 daily

NEW MAXIM'S #2

664 Jackson Street (between Grant and Kearny)
433-6753
Hours: 7—9 daily
Specialties: Coconut tarts, apple turnovers, ham and egg bau.

SUN WAH KUE

848 Washington Street (between Grant and Stockton)
982-3519
Hours: 7—7, closed Tuesday
Specialties: Apple pie, peanut cake.

THREE STAR BAKERY

1131 Grant Avenue (between Pacific and Broadway)
391-1133
Hours: 7:30—5:30 daily
Specialties: Deep-fried "cow ear" cookies (called "smackles"), strawberry cake.

UNCLE'S COFFEE SHOP

65 Waverly Place (near Clay)
982-1954
Hours: 9—8, closed Thursday
Specialties: Strawberry cake, dinner rolls.

GROCERY STORES

Chinese grocery stores, jammed with odd and exotic products, seem mystifying and bizarre and forbidding, but are well worth getting into. It takes some extra wandering around to find what you want, and you will have to accept being stared at (though politely), being crowded, reading labels, and taking chances. But when you do, you will find that there is a great variety of foods, prices are generally lower than anywhere else in town, vegetables are fresher, clerks are quite helpful, and shopping is fun once you get into the spirit of the thing. In fact, you will wonder why you hesitated in the first place.

One reason shopping in Chinatown is economical, besides a generally lower base price for most things, is that a lot of foods are sold loose, not prepackaged, so you only buy what you need right then; this also makes it easier to shop around for bargains or the best quality available.

There is also an interesting variety of brand-name goods available, many from Taiwan and Hong Kong and increasing amounts from mainland China, instead of the standard few brands that we've become accustomed to in American supermarkets. In the glossary, we've indicated some reliable brands, but don't hesitate to experiment; most sizes of packaged foods are small and inexpensive, so there's not much to lose, and we haven't come across anything terrible or substandard yet.

It's hard to tell from the outside just how extensive the stock in any of these stores is; the best way is to take a deep breath and plunge in — smiling.

Here are some shops that offer quality, value, and good selections. None accept checks or credit cards.

BROTHERS DISCOUNT MARKET

620 Pacific Avenue (between Grant and Kearny)
433-3437
Hours: 8–7 daily
Fresh fruits, vegetables, teas, cooking utensils, a large selection of canned and dried foods, low prices.

CHONG IMPORTS

838 Grant Avenue (between Washington and Clay)
982-1434
Hours: Mon–Sat 9:30–6, Sun noon–6
Dishes and cooking utensils, teas, canned and dried foods.

CHUCK LEE'S MARKET

1300 Powell Street (corner of Pacific)
421-8899
Hours: 8–7 daily
Fresh fruits and vegetables, teas, canned and dried foods.

HANG MEI COMPANY

155 Waverly Place (near Washington)
391-5170
Hours: 10–6 daily except holidays
Dishes and a good selection of canned and dried foods.

KAU SHING GROCERY COMPANY

1306 Stockton Street (between Vallejo and Broadway)
391-6344
Hours: 9–6 daily
Vegetables, fruits, canned and dried foods.

KENSON TRADING COMPANY

1251 Stockton Street (between Broadway and Pacific)
668-4433
Hours: 9–6 daily
A good selection of teas; dishes; canned, dried, and frozen foods.

MAY WAH TRADING COMPANY

1265 Stockton Street (near Broadway)
397-1527
Hours: 7–6 daily
Good vegetables and fruits; quite a few sweets and candies.

METRO FOOD COMPANY

641 Broadway (between Grant and Stockton)
982-1874
Hours: 9:30—6 daily
A large, well-lighted store, more like a supermarket, with a wide selection of packaged foods, including what seems like every Oriental noodle ever made; an extensive frozen-food section that includes quite exotic stuff; and dishes and cookware.

MOW FUNG COMPANY

733 Washington Street (near Grant)
982-6330, 982-1953
Hours: 7—4, closed Sunday
A very good selection of vegetables.

SUN TONG LEE

1351 Powell Street (near Broadway)
781-0728
Hours: 8:30—6 daily
Fresh fruits and vegetables, teas, and packaged foods.

TAI YICK TRADING COMPANY

1400 Powell Street (near Broadway)
986-0961
Hours: 9:30—6, closed Sunday
Good values in dishes, canned and dried foods.

WING SING CHONG COMPANY

1076 Stockton Street (near Jackson)
982-4174
Hours: 9—6, closed Wednesday
A good selection of dishes and cooking utensils, canned and dried foods.

WO SOON PRODUCE COMPANY

1210 Stockton Street (near Pacific)
989-2350
Hours: 9–6 daily
A good selection of vegetables; some other foods.

YING COMPANY

1120 Stockton Street (between Pacific and Jackson)
982-2188
Hours: 9:30–5, closed Sunday
A very good selection of clay pots of all shapes and sizes; dishes, cooking utensils, teas.

ORANGES

Orange Land is a fruit stand located at the corner of Stockton and Jackson streets for the past twenty-five years. It began by selling oranges, the favorite fruit of the Chinese, but now other fruits are offered as well. Purchases can be made here speedily and conveniently, with the clerks quickly filling and delivering orders to customers waiting at curbside. The success of Orange Land is due to the fact that the owner has always trucked in the sweetest oranges he could find, selling them at a reasonable price.

Oranges are held in very high esteem by the Chinese. Their bright color and sweet taste make them the perfect fruit for having around the house, especially at Chinese New Year. When visiting a friend's home, it is customary to bring oranges as a gesture of friendship.

BUTCHER SHOPS

Chinatown butcher shops tend to look like enclaves of the impoverished compared to the bulging meat cases of the average supermarket, but that is because they usually cut up and display only a little meat at a time; some haggling will generally bring out more for your inspection, and you can get meat cut to order. Prices for beef will generally be only a little less than elsewhere, but you may get a better cut for the money. The selection of pork, on the other hand, will be quite good, and so should the prices. Not all the butchers and clerks speak good English, but they usually have enough to negotiate, along with a little sign language.

CHUNG FAT COMPANY

921 Grant Avenue (near Washington)
421-4558
Hours: 8—7:30 daily
Chinese sausage, made on the premises.

GOLDEN GATE MEAT MARKET

1101 Stockton Street (near Jackson)
392-0940
Hours: 9—6 daily

HOP SANG MEAT MARKET

1199 Stockton Street (near Pacific)
982-2318
Hours: 9—6, closed Sunday

KWONG JOW SAUSAGE MANUFACTURING COMPANY

1157 Grant Avenue (near Broadway)
397-2562, 397-2563
Hours: Mon—Sat 9—5:30, Sun 9—4:30
Chinese sausage, made on the premises.

SHEW WO MEAT COMPANY

1151 Stockton Street (near Pacific)
982-7234
734 Jackson Street (between Grant and Stockton)
362-5842
Hours: (both locations) 8–6:30 daily

STOCKTON MEAT MARKET

1352 Stockton Street (near Vallejo)
421-0707
Hours: 9–6, closed Sunday and Wednesday

FISH, SHELLFISH, AND POULTRY MARKETS

The Chinese show their respect for fish by cooking it simply and by buying it as fresh as possible, often even alive, to be killed, cleaned, and scaled (after weighing, of course) on demand — one reason there always seems to be an extraordinary amount of activity going on in a Chinatown fish market. Fishmongers tend to be helpful and cooperative, but the pace can sometimes be a little frantic, so it's best not to be indecisive — if you see something you like or have something in mind, just start talking.

There is a species of fish often seen swimming in holding tanks, a freshwater fish called simply "blackfish." It is very popular with the Chinese (it has a fresh, almost sweet flavor), but it also has lots of treacherous, Y-shaped bones. If this doesn't bother you, eat it in a good light and chew thoroughly.

Prawns are sold in three sizes: small, medium, and large; the first two are most suitable for Chinese cooking, and less expensive than the largest ones. Bay shrimp are also available at some times of the year; the Chinese just boil them and toss with soy sauce and hot oil.

And of course, this is the place to come during crab season, since you can buy crabs live and kicking. If asked, the clerk will kill and clean them for you.

Poultry is always fresh, local, and more flavorful than the mass-produced supermarket specimens. Birds are also sold whole, which means more ingredients for the stockpot. Once again, prices are a little lower than elsewhere in town, and sales are by cash only.

CANTON MARKET

1135 Stockton Street (between Pacific and Jackson)
982-8600
Hours: 8—6 daily
Fresh fish, shellfish, and poultry.

DUPONT MARKET

1100 Grant Avenue (at Pacific)
986-3723
Hours: 8—5:30 daily
Fresh fish, shellfish, and poultry.

HONG KONG MARKET

1343 Powell Street (between Broadway and Pacific)
433-6313
Hours: 8—6 daily
Fish and shellfish only (no poultry).

HONG SANG MARKET

1136 Grant Avenue (near Broadway)
982-4145
Hours: 9:30—5:30 daily
Fresh fish, shellfish, and poultry.

LEE SANG FISH MARKET

1207 Stockton Street (between Pacific and Jackson)
989-4336
Hours: 8—6 daily
Fish and shellfish only (no poultry).

ON SANG POULTRY

1114 Grant Avenue (between Broadway and Pacific)
982-4694
Hours: 8—6 daily
Fresh fish, shellfish, and poultry.

SANG SANG MARKET

1143 Stockton Street (between Pacific and Jackson)
443-0403
Hours: 9–6 daily
Fish and shellfish only (no poultry).

SUN SANG MARKET

1205 Stockton Street (near Pacific)
989-3060
Hours: 8:30–5:30 daily
Poultry and prawns only (no fish or other shellfish).

NOODLES

NEW HONG KONG NOODLE FACTORY

874 Pacific Avenue (just below Powell)
982-2715
Hours: Mon—Sat 8—6, Sun 8—4
No checks or credit cards

Freshly made noodles are delightful, and this is the source, in Chinatown. In addition to fresh noodles, this family-operated store makes egg roll and won ton skins, pot sticker skins, dumpling (siu mai) skins, and suey gow skins. They also sell deep-fried "long-life noodles" (yee mein) and a variety of cookies. This is a very friendly place, and the owner himself may serve you, using an abacus to calculate your change. Until recently, you could watch the noodles being made, but the factory has been relocated to larger quarters, so this is now just a retail outlet.

Some of the noodles and wrappers you may find here and elsewhere in Chinatown are:

FRESH NOODLES

Chinese markets get fresh noodles every day, so they are often found on the counter instead of in the refrigerator. They are sold in one-pound packages, and come in different widths. The wider noodles are used in soup, and are not particularly satisfactory for chow mein. The fine noodles are used in soup, or with oyster sauce (lo mein). The medium width is used for pan-frying. Fresh noodles will keep for a week in the refrigerator, or for three months in the freezer. Defrost frozen noodles for several hours at room temperature before using. (Price: about 65¢ a pound.)

DEEP-FRIED NOODLES

These are called yee mein or "long-life noodles." They are already deep-fried and pressed into half-pound cakes about eight inches in diameter. They must be boiled before using in soups or gravies or for stir-frying. These are always served for good luck at Chinese birthday celebrations, usually in soup. They will keep for two weeks at room temperature. (Do not confuse these with the loose deep-fried so-called "chow mein noodles" resembling shoestring potatoes, which can be eaten as is.) (Price: about $1.25 per package.)

DUMPLING SKINS

These skins are about three inches in diameter, are thinner than pot sticker skins, and come over a hundred to a package, wrapped in parchment. They should be stored in a plastic bag. In the refrigerator, they will keep about a week, and frozen about two months. Frozen skins of all types should be thawed at least five hours at room temperature before using. (Price: about $1 a pound.)

EGG ROLL SKINS

A paper-thin skin, about six inches square, is available in one-pound parchment-wrapped packages of about twenty-five sheets — the number varies. An even thinner skin, sealed in a plastic bag (under the brand names of Ho Tai, Chinese Inn, Doll, or Menlo) is a little more work to separate, but makes a better, crisper egg roll. Leftover skins may be kept refrigerated for a week, or frozen for a few months. (Price: from $1 to $1.50 per pound.)

POT STICKER SKINS (KUO TEH)

These three-inch-diameter skins are especially made for pot stickers. They closely resemble dumpling skins, but are thicker, and come about forty skins to a sealed plastic package. Put them in a plastic bag, and refrigerate for one week or freeze for up to two months. (Price: about $1 per package.)

SUEY GOW SKINS

These skins are usually sold to restaurants and may not be available in grocery stores; they are sold at the noodle factory. They are four inches in diameter, and come about sixty to a parchment-wrapped package. They should be stored in a plastic bag, and will keep for a week in the refrigerator or up to two months in the freezer. (Price: about $1.25 per package.)

WON TON SKINS

A paper-thin noodle about 3½ inches square, which comes in parchment-wrapped one-pound packages (about eighty-five skins). They will keep for one week refrigerated, or may be frozen for two months. (Price: about $1 per pound.)

MISCELLANY

Most Chinese shops defy categorization, and will sell almost anything as long as there is a demand for it and room can be made for it. The many gift shops are a curious blend of utter schlock and exquisite goods, and there are some other places that bear firsthand investigation, especially those selling fabrics and jewelry. Maintaining our mostly culinary orientation, here are five offbeat places we like.

CHEW CHONG TAI & COMPANY

905 Grant Avenue (between Washington and Jackson)
982-0479
Hours: Mon—Sat 10—9, Sun 10—5
No checks or credit cards

This shop has the best assortment of Camel brand thermos bottles from Hong Kong, which are very well made and perfect for keeping hot tea that way. They also have an excellent selection of calligraphy brushes and inks, and other art supplies. Kits and toys, posters, and hand-carved ivory cigarette holders are also available.

CHINATOWN KITE SHOP

717 Grant Avenue (between Clay and Sacramento)
391-8217
Hours: 10—10 daily
Credit cards: MasterCard, Visa

The inside of this shop is a rainbow splash of colors in an improbable array of shapes bedecking walls and the ceiling: bird kites, box kites, tiger kites, goofy kites, and elegant kites, made of cloth and nylon and Mylar and good old-fashioned paper, which you can buy ready-made or to assemble. There is an especially good selection of Chinese kites, which seem far better gifts or souvenirs than knickknacks or dopey T-shirts.

LUN ON

771 Sacramento Street (between Grant and Kearny)
982-6152
Hours: Mon—Fri 10—5, Sat 10—4, closed Sunday
Credit cards: MasterCard, Visa

This shop features high-quality bamboo and rattan furniture and a good selection of blinds, as well as other woven-wood products, baskets, mats, screens, and bamboo poles; many of the rice paper screens have beautiful designs. They also do custom caning. Lun On has been in business since 1908, and the family that runs it is courteous and speaks good English.

QUON SHING COMPANY

118—20 Waverly Place (between Washington and Clay)
982-1088
Hours: 7—4:30, closed Sunday
No check or credit cards

From the street, it looks like just another produce market, but Quon Shing is the only place in Chinatown that makes its own candied fruits, and they are very good indeed, especially the candied winter melon, which is not too sweet but very refreshing. The candied coconut and ginger are also first rate. Around the time of Chinese New Year, you can also find dried sweetened lotus seeds, good as a snack or to sweeten tea for special occasions. The staff is very helpful.

THE WOK SHOP

804 Grant Avenue (between Washington and Clay)
989-3797
Hours: 10:30–10 daily
Credit cards: MasterCard, Visa

As you might guess, this narrow, cluttered shop sells a good
selection of woks, and also steamer baskets, cleavers, Chinese
cooking utensils of all sorts, other cooking utensils of all sorts,
and a lot of Chinese cookbooks to tell you how to use them, as
well as teapots, dishes, chopstick rests, cups, and an assortment
of different chopsticks — everything you need to cook Chinese
except the food. It must have taken a kind of genius to get this
much stuff organized into this little space.

A back room contains a variety of baskets and other woven
goods, including hats. There is also a selection of teas in attractive
boxes and canisters. The staff is quite helpful, and if you can't
find what you're looking for, either ask them or look up — what
you want might be hanging from the ceiling.

Some Chinatown Recipes

by Jennie Low

There have been quite a number of Chinese cookbooks published in the last decade; some try to adapt recipes to non-Chinese tastes, some try to preserve the purity of a region's cuisine and culture. Our selection represents a good cross-section of various styles and consists of dishes that are not difficult to make yet are a little out of the ordinary.

HONG KONG–STYLE TOMATO SOUP
STEAMED RICE
SZECHUAN SPICED NOODLES
SING CHOW RICE NOODLES
SHANGHAI NOODLES
FRIED DUMPLINGS WITH CHILI SAUCE
JENNIE'S SPARERIBS
LION'S HEADS
DEEP-FRIED PORK CUTLET
GINGER BEEF
KING DU BEEF
HUNAN BEEF
HOT AND SOUR BEEF
ALMOND CHICKEN
HOT SPICED CHICKEN
PINE NUT CHICKEN
CASHEW NUT PRAWNS AND SCALLOPS
PRAWNS IN SPICY BLACK BEAN SAUCE
STEAMED ROCK COD WITH SCALLIONS AND GINGER
SWEET POTATO BALLS

HONG KONG–STYLE TOMATO SOUP

Serves 4

2 medium tomatoes (½ lb.)*	*Seasoning*
	¼ tsp. salt
¼ lb. flank steak (or ground round)	¼ tsp. sugar
	1 tsp. white wine
1 potato (about 1 cup diced)	1 tsp. thin soy sauce
	1 tsp. cornstarch
1 stalk celery	
¼ yellow onion (about ¼ cup diced)	*Thickening mixture*
	2 tsp. cornstarch
4 cups chicken stock	mixed well with
2 eggs, beaten with a fork	2 tsp. cold water
2 green onions, finely chopped	2 tsp. sugar
	1 tbsp. dark soy sauce
	2 tsp. sesame oil

1. Dice tomatoes into ½-inch cubes.

2. Mince flank steak. Add seasoning ingredients and mix well. (A food processor may be used.)

3. Peel and dice potato into ½-inch cubes.

4. Peel strings from outside of celery, using a vegetable peeler. Dice into ½-inch cubes.

5. Dice yellow onion into ½-inch cubes.

6. Bring chicken stock to a boil in wok or deep saucepan. Add potato. Cover and cook for 10 minutes over high heat.

7. Add tomato, celery, yellow onion. Drop in minced flank steak a half teaspoonful at a time. Cover and cook for 2 minutes.

8. Add thickening mixture. Cook for 30 seconds.

9. Add beaten eggs in a circular motion while stirring soup. Eggs will cook very quickly, so be careful not to overcook.

10. Sprinkle with chopped green onions. Serve.

Advance preparation: Steps 1 through 7 may be done a few hours in advance and kept at room temperature.

* Buy fully ripe tomatoes for better flavor.

STEAMED RICE

Serves 4

2 cups raw long-grain
   rice *
3 cups cold water **

1. In a 2-quart saucepan, place raw rice. Wash 4 times. Drain off
   excess water.

2. Add cold water. Cover and bring to a boil on a small burner
   over high heat (it will take about 7 to 8 minutes).

3. Remove cover and continue to cook until water is absorbed
   (about 5 minutes).

4. Reduce heat as low as it will go. Cover and simmer for about
   10 minutes. Watch it carefully, for if it boils dry, rice will
   burn very easily. If not served immediately, it can remain on
   low heat for up to half an hour. (If rice should scorch, remove
   from heat immediately! Put a piece of bread on top of rice and
   cover. Bread will absorb the burned taste. Discard bread.
   Avoid serving rice that sticks to bottom of pot.)

* One cup raw rice makes 2 cups cooked rice.

** If using an electric rice cooker, reduce water to 2¾ cups, or
follow directions that came with cooker.

Note: The Chinese housewife has a unique way of measuring
water for the rice. She does not use a measuring cup for either the
rice or the water. She puts the rice in the pot, making sure the
rice surface is flat, places her forefinger upright so it barely
touches the rice surface, and adds water to barely cover the first
joint (approximately 1 inch above the rice surface). This method
works no matter how much rice is in the pot. However, the pot
has to have straight sides, and the size of the pot depends on the
amount of rice to be cooked. For 1 cup of rice, use a 1½-qt. pot;
for 2 cups, a 2-qt. pot, for 3 cups a 3-qt. pot, etc.

SZECHUAN SPICED NOODLES

Serves 4

¾ lb. lean pork butt (about
    1 cup sliced)
2 qt. water
1 lb. fresh Chinese noodles
2 tbsp. oil
½ cup chicken stock
    (to cook meat)
2½ cups chicken stock (for
    broth)
¾ lb. bean sprouts (1 cup)
    or 1 cup jícama, cut in
    julienne
2 green onions, finely
    chopped

Thickening mixture
¼ cup water
2 tbsp. cornstarch
1½ tbsp. dark soy sauce
1 tbsp. hoisin sauce
1½ tbsp. Japanese rice
    vinegar *or* 1¼ tbsp.
    white vinegar
1 tsp. crushed dried red
    chili pepper

Seasoning
¾ tsp. salt
½ tsp. sugar
1 tsp. thin soy sauce
1 tsp. oyster sauce
2 tsp. white wine
2 tsp. cornstarch

1. Trim fat from pork. Cut pork into julienne strips about
   ¼-by-1½ inches.

2. Add seasoning ingredients to pork and mix well.

3. Bring 2 qt. water to a boil. Add noodles. Cook, uncovered,
   for 2 minutes. Pour into colander. Rinse under cold water;
   drain. Set aside.

4. Mix ingredients listed under thickening mixture. Set aside.

5. Heat wok. Add oil and pork strips. Stir-fry for 2 minutes over
   high heat. Add ½ cup chicken stock. Cover and cook for 2
   minutes.

6. Meanwhile, bring 2½ cups chicken stock to a boil. Add
   noodles. Cook for 30 seconds. Remove from heat.

7. To pork mixture in step 5, add bean sprouts or jícama. Add
   thickening mixture. Cook for 30 seconds. Turn off heat.

8. Serve noodles in 4 individual serving bowls, each with about ½ cup chicken stock. Top each bowl of noodles with ¼ of pork mixture. Garnish with green onions. Mix ingredients before eating.

Note: This is not a noodle soup, but more of a noodle stew, because there is so little liquid.

Advance preparation: Steps 1 though 4 may be done the night before and refrigerated.

Variation: Chicken meat may be substituted for the pork, using the same cooking time.

SING CHOW RICE NOODLES

Serves 8

1 lb. rice sticks
   (py mei fun) *
2 qt. water
½ lb. pork butt
1 whole chicken breast
   (about 1 cup
   shredded meat)
1 lb. cabbage
4 tbsp. oil
⅓ cup chicken stock
¾ cup shredded bamboo
   shoots
1½ tbsp. curry powder **
1 tsp. salt
1 tsp. sugar
2 tsp. thin soy sauce
2 tbsp. oyster sauce
1½ tbsp. sesame oil
1 lb. bean sprouts

Seasoning
1½ tsp. salt
1 tsp. sugar
2 tsp. thin soy sauce
1 tbsp. oyster sauce
1 tbsp. white wine
1 tbsp. cornstarch

1. Soak rice sticks in warm water to cover for 20 minutes. Pour into a colander and drain.

2. Bring 2 qt. water to a boil. Add rice sticks and cook for 30 seconds, uncovered. (Don't wait for water to return to a boil!) Pour into colander. Rinse under cold water. Drain.

3. Trim fat from pork. Cut into thin strips juilenne style.

4. Remove skin from chicken. Cut meat into thin strips julienne style.

5. Add seasoning ingredients to pork and chicken. Mix well.

6. Shred cabbage into 1½-by-½-inch strips.

7. Heat wok. Add 1 tbsp. oil, pork, and chicken, and stir-fry for 2 minutes over high heat. Add chicken stock and shredded bamboo shoots. Cover and cook for 2 minutes.

8. Add shredded cabbage to chicken mixture. Mix well and cook, uncovered, for 1 minute. Remove from wok and set aside.

9. Rinse and stir rice sticks under cold water; drain. (They must be slightly moist so they won't stick together when stir-fried.) Immediately heat wok. Add 1½ tbsp. oil and curry powder. Cook about 15 seconds. Add half of rice sticks and stir-fry over high heat for 2 minutes. Sprinkle in ½ tsp. salt, ½ tsp. sugar, 1 tsp. thin soy sauce, 1 tbsp. oyster sauce, and ¾ tbsp. sesame oil. Mix thoroughly. Add half of bean sprouts and half of meat and vegetable mixture. Mix well. Remove from wok to a warm oven while you repeat this procedure with remaining rice sticks, meat, vegetables, and bean sprouts.

Advance preparation: Steps 1 through 8 may be done a few hours in advance and kept at room temperature.

Serving suggestion: This makes an excellent one-dish luncheon. Leftovers may be reheated in a microwave oven, or in a dry (no oil) Teflon-lined frying pan.

* Be sure to buy rice sticks labeled "Py Mei Fun." There is another rice noodle labeled "Lai Fun," which is used for soup only.

** For this recipe, Madras brand curry is recommended. It is available in any Chinese grocery store.

SHANGHAI NOODLES

Serves 5

2 qt. water
1 lb. fresh Chinese noodles
1 tbsp. chili paste with
   garlic *
1 tbsp. sesame seed
   paste **
1 tbsp. white wine
1 tbsp. thin soy sauce
1 tbsp. oil
3 eggs, beaten with a fork
2 green onions, finely
   chopped

Sauce
⅓ cup chicken stock
1 tbsp. sesame oil
1½ tbsp. oyster sauce
1 tbsp. sesame seed paste

1. Bring 2 qt. water to a boil. Add noodles and stir to separate.
   Cook uncovered for 2 minutes. Pour into a colander. Rinse
   under cold water. Drain. Place on serving platter immediately. (If noodles get dry, it is difficult to mix in seasonings.)

2. Mix together chili paste with garlic, sesame seed paste, white
   wine, and thin soy sauce. Pour over noodles. Mix well. Chill
   for 4 hours.

3. Mix together ingredients for sauce. Mix well. Set aside.

4. Heat frying pan (preferably Teflon-lined). Add ½ tbsp. oil.
   Add half of beaten egg. Rotate pan to spread egg into a very
   thin "pancake." Cook until set. Turn and cook other side
   briefly. Remove from pan. Repeat this procedure with
   remaining oil and beaten egg. Cut into fine strips.

5. When noodles have chilled for 4 hours, pour sauce (from
   step 3) over noodles. Mix well. Top with green onions and
   egg strips. Serve.

* Lan Chi brand chili paste with garlic comes in an 8-oz. jar,
available in any Chinese grocery. Refrigerated, it will keep for 2
years.

** Lan Chi brand sesame seed paste also comes in an 8-oz. jar,
and will keep for 2 years in the refrigerator.

FRIED DUMPLINGS WITH CHILI SAUCE

Makes about 34

1 lb. lean ground pork
2 green onions,
   finely chopped
2 tsp. ginger,
   finely chopped
2 tbsp. Tientsin preserved
   vegetables, rinsed
   and chopped *
1 cup finely chopped
   cabbage
1 pkg. pot sticker skins
3 cups oil for deep-frying

Seasoning
½ tsp. salt
½ tsp. sugar
2 tsp. thin soy sauce
2 tsp. oyster sauce
1 tbsp. white wine
1½ tbsp. cornstarch
1 egg

Sealing mixture
1 tbsp. flour mixed well
   with
2 tbsp. cold water

Sauce
¾ cup chicken stock
¼ cup thin soy sauce
¼ cup Japanese seasoned
   rice vinegar **
2 tsp. oyster sauce
2 tsp. hot oil ***

Garnish
1½ tbsp. finely chopped
   garlic
3 green onions, finely
   chopped

1. Place ground pork, 2 chopped green onions, ginger, and preserved vegetables on chopping board. Mix and chop with cleaver until thoroughly combined. (A food processor may be used for this step.)

2. Add seasoning ingredients. Mix thoroughly. Add chopped cabbage and mix well again.

3. Place ¾ tbsp. pork mixture on center of a pot sticker skin. Brush sealing mixture halfway around edge of pot sticker skin. Fold in half, sealing edges by pressing them together tightly. Set pot sticker on its straight edge on a platter and press firmly to form a flat base. Fill remaining skins in same way.

4. Heat oil to 325°. Deep-fry approximately one third of pot stickers (11) at a time, keeping them warm afterward in a 250° oven.

5. While pot stickers are deep-frying, prepare sauce. Bring chicken stock to a boil. Turn off heat and add remaining ingredients. Mix well. Set aside.

6. Place pot stickers on a serving platter. Garnish with chopped garlic and 3 chopped green onions. Pour sauce over and serve immediately. (As long as pot stickers are hot, sauce need not be boiling.)

Advance preparation: Pot stickers may be prepared and frozen in a tightly sealed container for up to 3 months. They may be deep-fried without thawing.

* Tientsin preserved vegetables come in clay pots (and sometimes in jars). To store, cover the clay pot with foil, or remove to a covered jar, and refrigerate. They will keep for 2 years.

** Marukan brand Japanese rice vinegar is available in a "seasoned gourmet" style (orange label) as well as the "genuine brewed" style (green label). We think the additional flavor improves this dish, but regular rice vinegar may be used.

*** To make hot oil, heat ½ cup oil over high heat for 2 minutes. Drop in 1 or 2 pieces of crushed dried red chili pepper to test oil temperature. (If they turn dark, let oil cool a few minutes.) Add 2 tsp. crushed dried red chili pepper. Let cool. Put in a glass container and let stand at least 1 week before using. (During this time, chili pepper will settle to the bottom of jar.) Oil will keep for several months at room temperature, and may be added to noodles or other dishes for a spicy taste. For a less spicy dish, substitute sesame oil for hot oil in sauce mixture.

JENNIE'S SPARE RIBS

Serves 5

2 lb. pork spareribs
2 qt. water
1 tbsp. oil
2 tsp. finely chopped garlic
½ cup cold water
2 tbsp. white wine
2½ tbsp. white vinegar or
   cider vinegar
3 tbsp. sugar
4 tbsp. dark or thin soy
   sauce
2 green onions, finely
   chopped

1. Have your butcher cut spareribs into strips 1½ inches wide.
    Cut rib bones apart; trim off fat.

2. Bring 2 qt. water to a boil. Parboil meat for 3 minutes. Drain
    well.

3. Heat wok (or saucepan). Add oil, garlic, and spareribs.
    Stir-fry for 3 minutes over high heat. Add ½ cup cold water,
    white wine, vinegar, sugar, and soy sauce. Bring to a fast boil.
    Reduce to medium heat. Cover and cook for 40 minutes.
    (Check liquid occasionally. Add more water if necessary.)

4. Remove to a platter (including liquid). Garnish with green
    onions. Serve.

Advance preparation: The entire recipe may be prepared in advance
and refrigerated. It keeps well for several days. It may be kept
warm in a covered casserole in a low oven for up to an hour.

Serving suggestion: This dish goes well with steamed rice. (The
juice is very tasty.)

Variation: Substitute raw chicken parts. Leave thighs and drumsticks whole; cut whole breast into 6 equal pieces. Omit the
parboiling. Beef ribs cut into 2-inch pieces are also delicious
cooked this way (without parboiling). Cooking time remains the
same for both variations.

LION'S HEADS

Serves 5

1 lb. lean ground pork
1½ lb. Napa cabbage
2 tbsp. Cantonese-style
  bean sauce *
1 tbsp. sugar
2 cups oil for deep frying
1½ cups chicken stock
2 green onions, finely
  chopped

Thickening mixture
1½ tbsp. cornstarch mixed
  well with
3 tbsp. cold water

Seasoning
1 tsp. salt
1 tsp. sugar
1 tbsp. thin soy sauce
1 tbsp. white wine
1 tbsp. oyster sauce
2½ tbsp. cornstarch
1 large egg

1. Add seasoning ingredients to ground pork and mix well.

2. Form into meatballs about 2 inches in diameter. (You should have 5 meatballs.)

3. Cut Napa cabbage into 2-inch pieces.

4. Mash bean sauce into a paste. Add 1 tbsp. sugar and mix well.

5. Heat 2 cups oil in wok to 325°. Add 3 meatballs. Deep-fry until golden brown (about 1½ minutes), turn, and deep-fry the other side until golden brown (about 1½ minutes). Remove and drain on paper towels. Repeat procedure with remaining meatballs.

6. Using a wok or large saucepan, add chicken stock, bean sauce mixture, deep-fried meatballs, and cabbage. Bring to a fast boil. Reduce to medium heat, cover, and cook for 20 minutes. Stir occasionally, being careful not to break the meatballs.

7. Add thickening mixture. Cook for 30 seconds. (This should make a thick gravy. Sometimes it is necessary to add additional thickening mixture.)

8. Remove to serving dish. Top with green onions. Serve.

Advance preparation: Steps 1 through 6 may be done up to 6 hours in advance and kept at room temperature. Bring quickly to a boil before adding the thickening mixture.

* Buy Koon Chun brand bean sauce (Cantonese-style bean sauce), not Szechuan-style bean sauce. This is not meant to be a spicy dish.

Note: There's no need to kill a lion to make this dish. "Lion's head" is merely a Chinese euphemism for a meatball.

DEEP-FRIED PORK CUTLETS

Serves 4

1 lb. pork cutlets
2 cups oil for deep-frying

Seasoning
½ tsp. salt
½ tsp. sugar
1 tsp. thin soy sauce
1 tsp. oyster sauce

Batter
½ cup cornstarch
¼ cup cold water

Sauce
¼ cup juice from canned peaches, pears, or fruit cocktail
2½ tsp. Worcestershire sauce
2 tsp. white wine
1 tsp. sesame oil

Thickening mixture
1 tsp. cornstarch mixed well with
2 tsp. cold water

1. On a chopping board, pound pork cutlets with side of a cleaver to tenderize. Cut into strips approximately 2-by-1 inch.
2. Add seasoning ingredients to pork strips and mix well.
3. Prepare batter by mixing ingredients listed.
4. Combine sauce ingredients. Bring to a boil and add thickening mixture. Set aside.

5. Heat oil to 325° in wok. Dip pork strips in batter, one at a time, allowing excess batter to drain back into bowl. Draw pork strip across edge of bowl to remove last bit of excess batter and drop into hot oil. Continue this procedure until all strips are coated. Allow to deep-fry approximately 4 minutes. Drain on paper towels. Remove to a platter and keep warm while reheating sauce.

6. Reheat sauce to boiling (being careful not to let it boil away). Pour over pork and serve immediately.

Advance preparation: Steps 1 through 4 may be done ahead and kept at room temperature.

GINGER BEEF

Serves 5

1 lb. flank steak
2 tbsp. oil
1 tbsp. slivered ginger *
  (about ¾ inch long)
3 green onions, slivered
2 eggs, beaten with a fork

Thickening mixture
½ cup chicken stock mixed
  well with
1 tbsp. cornstarch
1 tbsp. sesame oil
2 tsp. dark soy sauce

Marinade
1 tsp. salt
½ tsp. sugar
1 tsp. thin soy sauce
1 tbsp. white wine
1 tbsp. oyster sauce
1 tbsp. cornstarch
Dash pepper

1. Cut flank steak into 3 equal strips with grain of meat. Cut each strip crosswise into thin slices.

2. Sprinkle marinade ingredients over beef. Mix well and marinate for 1 hour.

3. Heat wok. Add oil, marinated beef, and slivered ginger. Stir-fry for 3 minutes over high heat.

4. Add green onions and thickening mixture. Cook for 30 seconds, stirring occasionally.

5. Add beaten egg. Cook 30 seconds (do not overcook!). Serve.

Advance preparation: Steps 1 and 2 may be done the night before. Refrigerate.

Note: This dish goes very well with steamed rice. It is served in most Cantonese restaurants and is a very popular dish in the Chinese home. It is quick, easy, and delicious.

* The amount of ginger may be reduced to 1 tsp. if desired.

KING DU BEEF

Serves 6

1 lb. flank steak
1 medium-sized head
   cauliflower
3½ tbsp. oil
½ tsp. salt
½ tsp. sugar
¾ cup chicken stock
2 cloves of garlic, finely
   chopped
7 dried whole red chili
   peppers
1 tbsp. hoisin sauce
2 green onions, slivered

Marinade
½ tsp. baking soda
1 tsp. warm water
½ tsp. salt
½ tsp. sugar
2 tsp. dark soy sauce
1 tsp. thin soy sauce
1 tbsp. oyster sauce
1 tbsp. cornstarch
1 tbsp. sesame oil
1½ tbsp. white wine
Dash pepper

Thickening mixture
2 tsp. cornstarch mixed
   well with
2 tsp. cold water
2 tsp. dark soy sauce

1. Cut flank steak lengthwise into 3 equal strips approximately 1½ inches wide. Cut each strip across grain slantwise into thin slices approximately ¼ inch thick, and 1½-by-1½ inches.

2. To marinate, mix baking soda with warm water (see marinade) and add to meat. (This helps to tenderize meat.) Add remaining marinade ingredients. Marinate at least 8 hours or overnight.

3. Remove core of cauliflower and discard. Break off florets into 2-inch pieces.

4. Heat wok. Add 1 tbsp. oil. Stir-fry cauliflower for 2 minutes over high heat.

5. Add ½ tsp. salt, ½ tsp. sugar, and ¾ cup chicken stock. Cover and cook for 4 minutes over high heat.

6. Prepare thickening mixture. Add to cauliflower and cook 30 seconds. Remove from wok and keep warm in the oven.

7. Heat wok. Add 2½ tbsp. oil and chopped garlic. Stir-fry for 30 seconds.

8. Add whole red peppers, hoisin sauce, and beef. Stir-fry for 3 minutes over high heat. (If meat is not sufficiently cooked, increase cooking time.) Whole red peppers may be left in, for added color, or removed.

9. Add slivered green onions. Stir well.

10. If necessary, reheat cauliflower for 30 seconds. Place on a serving platter. Pour cooked beef over, as a topping. Serve.

Advance preparation: Steps 1 through 3 may be done a day or so in advance and refrigerated.

Variation: Asparagus, bok choy, or broccoli may be substituted for the cauliflower. Adjust cooking times as follows: in step 5, cook for 3 minutes, uncovered, over high heat.

HUNAN BEEF

Serves 4

1 lb. flank steak
½ lb. broccoli
2 tbsp. oil for stir-frying
1½ tsp. finely chopped
  garlic
¾ yellow onion (1 cup),
  thinly sliced
4 green onions, slivered

Thickening mixture
½ cup chicken stock mixed
  well with
1 tbsp. cornstarch

Seasoning
1 tsp. salt
½ tsp. sugar
1 tsp. thin soy sauce
1 tbsp. oyster sauce
1¼ tbsp. cornstarch
Dash pepper

Sauce
2 tsp. Kimlan satay paste *
2 tsp. hoisin sauce
1 tbsp. sesame oil

1. Cut flank steak with grain of meat into 3 equal strips about 1½ inches wide. Cut each strip across grain into thin slices.

2. Add seasoning ingredients to beef and mix well.

3. Peel off tough outer part of broccoli stalks. Cut stalks in half lengthwise, then cut diagonally into very thin slices about 1½ inches long. Cut florets into very thin slices.

4. To make sauce, stir satay paste well before measuring. Mix together sauce ingredients. Mix well and set aside.

5. Heat wok. Add oil, garlic, and flank steak. Stir-fry over high heat for 2 minutes. Add yellow onion, broccoli, and green onions. Stir-fry for 1 minute.

6. Add sauce. Mix well.

7. Add thickening mixture. Cook for 30 seconds. Serve.

Advance preparation: Steps 1 through 4 may be done the night before and refrigerated.

Variation: Substitute snow peas or bell pepper for broccoli, using same cooking time.

* Kimlan satay paste comes in a 5-oz. jar and will keep in the refrigerator for 2 years.

HOT AND SOUR BEEF

Serves 4

1 lb. flank steak
½ can (19-oz. size) bamboo
    shoots * *or* about 1 cup
    jícama, cut in julienne
2 carrots
2 tbsp. oil for stir-frying
4 green onions, slivered
½ cup chicken stock

Marinade
1 tsp. salt
½ tsp. sugar
1½ tbsp. white wine
1 tsp. thin soy sauce
1 tbsp. oyster sauce
1¼ tbsp. cornstarch
Dash pepper

Sauce
1 tbsp. chili paste with
    garlic **
2 tbsp. Japanese rice
    vinegar *or* 1½ tbsp.
    white vinegar
1 tbsp. white wine
1 tbsp. sugar
1 tbsp. oyster sauce
1 tbsp. sesame oil

1. Cut flank steak with grain of meat into 3 equal strips about
   1½ inches wide. Cut each strip across grain into thin slices.

2. Add marinade to beef and mix well. Marinate for 1 hour or
   overnight. (If necessary, marinating time may be omitted.)

3. Slice bamboo shoots into julienne-style strips. If using jícama,
   peel off skin and slice into julienne-style strips.

4. Peel carrots and cut diagonally into very thin slices.

5. Mix together sauce ingredients. Set aside.

6. Heat wok. Add oil, flank steak, and carrot. Stir-fry for 3
   minutes over high heat. Add green onions and bamboo shoots
   or jícama. Mix well.

7. Add chicken stock. Bring to a fast boil.

8. Add sauce. Mix well. Cook for 30 seconds. Serve.

Advance preparation: Steps 1 through 4 may be done the night before and refrigerated.

* Buy Companion or Ma Ling brand winter bamboo shoots in water if possible. They have a better texture than regular bamboo shoots. Remaining bamboo shoots will keep in the refrigerator for up to 2 weeks. Place in a covered container with cold water. Change the water every 2 days.

** Lan Chi brand chili paste with garlic comes in an 8-oz. jar, available in any Chinese market. It will keep in the refrigerator for 2 years.

ALMOND CHICKEN

Serves 4

1 whole chicken breast
    (about 1 cup cut up)
2 cups oil for deep frying
½ cup blanched almonds
1 stalk celery
½ yellow onion
1 carrot
3 tbsp. oil for stir-frying
1 cup fresh mushrooms,
    diced in ½-inch cubes
¼ tsp. salt
¼ tsp. sugar
1 cup chicken stock
¾ cup diced bamboo
    shoots (about ½-inch
    cubes) *
2 green onions, cut in
    ½-inch lengths

Seasoning
½ tsp. salt
½ tsp. sugar
1 tsp. thin soy sauce
2 tsp. oyster sauce
1 tbsp. white wine
2 tsp. cornstarch

Thickening mixture
1 tbsp. cornstarch mixed
    well with
2 tbsp. cold water
1 tbsp. dark soy sauce
1 tbsp. sesame oil

1. Skin and bone chicken. Cut into ½-inch cubes.
2. Add seasoning ingredients to chicken and mix well.

3. Heat 1 cup oil to 300°. Put nuts into strainer and deep-fry in hot oil until golden brown (about 2 minutes). Take care not to burn! They brown very rapidly. Drain on paper towels.

4. Peel strings from outside of celery, using a vegetable peeler. Dice in ½-inch cubes.

5. Remove skin from yellow onion. Dice into ½-inch cubes.

6. Peel and dice carrot into ½-inch cubes.

7. Heat wok. Add 1 tbsp. oil, celery, yellow onion, and fresh mushrooms and stir-fry for 2 minutes over high heat. Add ¼ tsp. salt and ¼ tsp. sugar. Remove from wok and set aside.

8. Heat wok. Add 2 tbsp. oil and chicken. Stir-fry for 2 minutes over high heat.

9. Add chicken stock, bamboo shoots, and carrot. Cover and cook for 3 minutes.

10. Add celery mixture and green onions. Mix thoroughly.

11. Add thickening mixture. Cook for 30 seconds.

12. Remove from heat. Add deep-fried almonds. Mix well and serve.

Advance preparation: Steps 1 through 9 may be done a few hours ahead and stored at room temperature.

Variation: Cashew nuts may be substituted for almonds.

* Buy water-packed winter bamboo shoots in a can.

HOT SPICED CHICKEN

Serves 4

1½ lb. chicken thighs
  (about 2 cups chicken
  meat)
2 carrots
1 yellow onion
2 tbsp. oil
2 tsp. garlic, finely
  chopped
2 tsp. ginger, finely
  chopped
½ cup chicken stock
3 green onions, slivered

Seasoning
1 tsp. salt
1 tsp. sugar
2 tsp. thin soy sauce
1 tbsp. oyster sauce
1 tbsp. white wine
1 tbsp. cornstarch

Sauce
1 tbsp. hoisin sauce
1 tbsp. catsup
1½ tsp. dark soy sauce
1 tsp. crushed dried red
  chili pepper *
1 tbsp. sesame oil

1. Skin and bone chicken. Cut into strips about ½-by-1½ inches. Add seasoning ingredients to chicken and mix well.

2. Peel carrots and cut diagonally into thin slices.

3. Peel yellow onion and cut into ¼-inch wedges.

4. Combine sauce ingredients. Mix well and set aside.

5. Heat wok. Add oil, chopped garlic, ginger, and chicken. Stir-fry over high heat for 3 minutes. Add carrot, yellow onion, and chicken stock. Cover and cook for 2 minutes.

6. Add sauce and slivered green onions. Mix thoroughly and serve.

Advance preparation: Steps 1 through 5 may be done in advance. Reheat for 30 seconds before adding sauce.

Variation: Mushrooms and snow peas may be substituted for carrot and yellow onion. Add after step 5 and cook for 30 seconds.

* This may be reduced or omitted if you prefer a less spicy dish.

PINE NUT CHICKEN

Serves 4

1 whole chicken breast
   (about 1 cup chicken
   meat)
1½ cups oil for deep-frying
⅓ cup pine nuts
2 green onions
2½ tbsp. oil
1½ tsp. finely chopped
   garlic
⅓ cup chicken stock
½ cup diced yellow onion

Marinade
½ tsp. salt
½ tsp. sugar
1 tsp. thin soy sauce
2 tsp. oyster sauce
1 tbsp. white wine
2 tsp. cornstarch

Sauce
1½ tsp. sesame seed paste *
1 tsp. hoisin sauce

1. Skin and bone chicken breast. Cut into 1½-by-½-inch pieces.

2. Add marinade to chicken and mix well. Marinate for 1 hour or overnight.

3. Heat 1½ cups oil to 300°. Deep-fry pine nuts in a strainer until golden brown (approximately 2 minutes). Caution: Do not let them burn. They will go from golden brown to dark brown in just a few seconds. Drain off excess oil. Drain on a paper towel.

4. Cut green onions into ½-inch lengths.

5. To make sauce, before measuring out sesame seed paste, mix thoroughly to recombine oil and paste. Combine sesame seed paste and hoisin sauce in a small container. Mix thoroughly and set aside.

6. Heat wok. Add 2½ tbsp. oil, garlic, and chicken. Stir-fry over high heat for 3 minutes.

7. Add chicken stock. Cover and cook for 3 minutes.

8. Add green onions, yellow onion, and sauce. Cook for 30 seconds. Remove from heat. Add pine nuts. Serve.

Advance preparation: Pine nuts may be deep-fried up to 2 weeks in advance and stored in a closed container. Steps 1, 2, 4, and 5 may be done the night before and refrigerated.

* Lan Chi brand sesame seed paste comes in an 8-oz. jar. It will keep, refrigerated, for 2 years.

CASHEW NUT PRAWNS AND SCALLOPS

Serves 4

1½ cups oil for deep-frying
¾ cup raw cashew nuts
½ lb. raw prawns (medium sized preferred)
½ lb. fresh scallops
2 stalks celery
1 carrot
3 green onions
2 tbsp. oil for stir-frying
1 can (15 oz.) straw mushrooms, rinsed and drained

Seasoning
½ tsp. salt
½ tsp. sugar
1 tsp. thin soy sauce
1 tbsp. white wine
2 tsp. cornstarch
Dash pepper

Thickening mixture
½ cup chicken stock
1 tbsp. cornstarch
1 tbsp. dark soy sauce
1 tbsp. oyster sauce
1 tbsp. sesame oil
1 tsp. sugar

1. Heat 1½ cups oil to 300°. Deep-fry cashew nuts in a strainer until golden brown (about 2 minutes). Caution: Do not let them burn. They will go from golden brown to dark brown in just a few seconds. Drain off excess oil. Drain on a paper towel.

2. Shell, devein, wash, and drain prawns. (If using jumbo prawns, cut in half lengthwise.)

3. Cut scallops into pieces about 1½-by-½ inches.

4. Add seasoning ingredients to prawns and scallops. Mix well.

5. Peel outside of celery stalks with a vegetable peeler to remove strings. Cut celery into 1½-inch pieces. Cut each piece into strips julienne style.

6. Peel carrot and cut diagonally into thin slices.

7. Cut green onions into ½-inch pieces.

8. Combine ingredients listed under thickening mixture. Mix well; set aside.

9. Heat wok. Add 2 tbsp. oil, prawns, and scallops. Stir-fry for 2 minutes over high heat. Add straw mushrooms, celery, carrot, and green onions. Stir-fry for 1 minute more.

10. Add thickening mixture. Cook for 1 minute. Remove from heat.

11. Add deep-fried cashew nuts and serve.

Advance preparation: Step 1 may be done up to 2 weeks in advance and stored in a closed container. Steps 2 through 4 may be done a few hours in advance and refrigerated. Steps 5 through 8 may be done a few hours in advance and kept at room temperature.

Variations: You may substitute almonds for cashew nuts. You may also make this dish using 1 lb. scallops or 1 lb. prawns. Fresh mushrooms may be used instead of straw mushrooms, and snow peas instead of celery.

PRAWNS IN SPICY BLACK BEAN SAUCE

Serves 4

1 lb. raw prawns (medium sized preferred)	*Seasoning*
	½ tsp. salt
2½ tbsp. salted black beans *	1 tsp. thin soy sauce
	2 tsp. cornstarch
1 tbsp. sugar	Dash pepper
¾ tsp. crushed dried red chili pepper **	
1½ tbsp. oil	*Thickening mixture*
2 tsp. finely chopped garlic	½ cup chicken stock
1 cup sliced fresh mushrooms	1 tbsp. cornstarch
	1 tbsp. white wine
1 green onion, finely chopped	1 tbsp. sesame oil
	1 tbsp. oyster sauce

1. Shell, devein, wash, and drain prawns. (If using jumbo prawns, cut in half lengthwise.)

2. Add seasoning ingredients to prawns. Mix well.

3. Wash black beans twice. Mash into a paste. Add sugar and crushed red chili pepper. Mix well.

4. Combine ingredients for thickening mixture. Mix well. Set aside.

5. Heat wok. Add oil and garlic. Stir-fry for 30 seconds. Add black bean mixture, mushrooms, and prawns. Stir-fry over high heat for 2 minutes.

6. Add thickening mixture and green onion. Cook, uncovered, for 1 minute. Serve.

Advance preparation: Steps 1 through 3 may be done the night before and refrigerated. Step 4 may be done several hours in advance and kept at room temperature.

* Salted black beans come in a box or in a plastic bag, not in a can. (Do not confuse with canned bean sauce.) They will keep in the refrigerator for 2 years.

** This amount makes a moderately spicy dish. It may be increased or decreased to taste.

PRAWNS IN HOT GARLIC SAUCE

Serves 4

¾ lb. raw prawns (medium sized preferred)
1½ tbsp. oil
2 tsp. finely chopped garlic
1 green onion, chopped

Seasoning
¼ tsp. salt
1½ tsp. cornstarch
Dash pepper

Sauce
1½ tsp. chili paste with garlic *
1½ tbsp. catsup
1¼ tbsp. oyster sauce
1 tbsp. sugar
2 tbsp. white wine
1½ tbsp. sesame oil

1. Shell, devein, wash, and drain prawns. (If using jumbo prawns, cut in half lengthwise.)

2. Add seasoning ingredients to prawns and mix well.

3. Mix together sauce ingredients. Set aside.

4. Heat wok. Add oil and garlic. Stir-fry for 30 seconds. Add prawns. Stir-fry for 2 minutes over high heat.

5. Add sauce. Cook, uncovered, for 1 minute.

6. Remove to serving platter. Garnish with green onion. Serve.

Advance preparation: Steps 1 through 3 may be done the night before and refrigerated.

Variation: Any firm white fish (rock cod, sturgeon, halibut, red snapper, etc.), scallops, or even squid may be substituted, using the same cooking time.

* Lan Chi brand chili paste with garlic comes in an 8-oz. jar, available in any Chinese market. It will keep, refrigerated, for 2 years. If a spicier dish is desired, increase the amount to 2 tsp.

STEAMED ROCK COD WITH SCALLIONS AND GINGER

Serves 4

1½ lb. fresh rock cod steak (1½ inches thick)	*Seasoning*
	1 tsp. salt
1½ tbsp. slivered fresh ginger	1 tsp. sugar
	1½ tbsp. white wine
3 tbsp. oil	2 tsp. dark soy sauce
3 green onions, slivered	Dash pepper
1 tbsp. thin soy sauce	

1. Wash fish. Put in a shallow dish or stainless steel pie plate.

2. Sprinkle seasoning ingredients over fish. Add half of slivered ginger over fish (reserve other half for step 5).

3. Add water to wok. Place a steamer plate in wok (water level should be about ½ inch below steamer plate). Bring water to a boil. Place dish containing fish on steamer plate, cover, and cook for 20 minutes over high heat. (If fish steak is only 1 inch thick, reduce cooking time to 15 minutes; if ½ inch thick, steam for 10 minutes.) Test to see if fish is cooked. (Press with a chopstick. If chopstick penetrates, fish is done.)

4. During last minute of cooking, heat 3 tbsp. oil in a small saucepan for 1 minute over high heat. (It must be so hot it sizzles when poured over fish.)

5. Remove dish containing fish from wok. Sprinkle reserved slivered ginger and slivered green onions over fish. Pour hot oil and then soy sauce over fish. Serve immediately.

Variation: You may substitute fillets of perch, sand dabs, red snapper, sturgeon, black bass, or striped bass for rock cod. Whole fish (about 2 lb.) may also be used; in either case, judge the cooking time by the above standards.

SWEET POTATO BALLS

Makes about 24

1¼ lb. sweet potatoes
4 tbsp. sugar
½ cup flour
1 large egg
⅓ tsp. cinnamon *
⅓ tsp. nutmeg *
2 cups oil for deep-frying
1 tbsp. powdered sugar

1. Peel and wash sweet potatoes. Cut into quarters. Place on a pie plate. Steam in a wok until soft (about 15 minutes).
2. Mash while hot. Let cool slightly.
3. Stir in sugar, flour, egg, cinnamon, and nutmeg. Mix thoroughly with a spoon.
4. Using about 1 tablespoon mixture, form into small balls.
5. Heat oil to 325°. Drop about 6 potato balls into hot oil and fry until light brown (about 2 minutes). Drain on a paper towel. Sprinkle with powdered sugar. Repeat procedure with remaining potato balls. Serve hot or cold.

Advance preparation: Steps 1 through 4 may be done a few days in advance and refrigerated.

* Amount of cinnamon and nutmeg will depend upon your taste and the pungency of your spices.

About the Authors

Brian St. Pierre grew up around his family's restaurant business near Boston. A professional food and wine writer, he is currently Public Relations Director of Wine Institute in San Francisco, author of three books (including *The Flavor of North Beach*), and a charter member of the Society of Wine Educators. His extensive professional travels have provided opportunities to wield chopsticks in Chinese restaurants in places as diverse as Australia, Panama, France, and Canada; he has been happiest close to Grant Avenue.

Jennie Low, a native of Hong Kong, came to the United States as a young girl to go to school. After marrying she became more and more interested in developing her Chinese cooking skills until she was able to duplicate the delicious dishes of Chinatown's master chefs. She has taught Chinese cooking for sixteen years, is the author of two cookbooks, *Chopstick, Cleaver and Wok* and *Jennie Low's Szechuan Cookbook,* and coauthor of a restaurant guide, *The Chinese Restaurant Experience.*